THE KEYBOARD SCALE MANUAL

BY LEONARD VOGLER

A COMPLETE GUIDE TO SCALES. SPECIALLY DESIGNED KEYBOARD DIAGRAMS COMBINED WITH STANDARD NOTATION MAKE ANY SCALE EASY TO LEARN. INCLUDES BASIC SCALE THEORY AS WELL AS FINGERING PATTERNS FOR ALL MAJOR, MINOR, AND MODAL SCALES. A MUST FOR ALL KEYBOARD PLAYERS.

AMSCO PUBLICATIONS
NEW YORK / LONDON / SYDNEY

Interior design and layout by Len Vogler
edited by Amy Appleby

This book Copyright © 1992 by Amsco Publications,
A Division of Music Sales Corporation, New York, NY.

Order No. AM 76225
US International Standard Book Number: 0.8256.1249.7
UK International Standard Book Number: 0.7119.1907.0

Exclusive Distributors:
Music Sales Corporation
257 Park Avenue South, New York, NY 10010 USA
Music Sales Limited
8/9 Frith Street, London W1V 5TZ England
Music Sales Pty. Limited
120 Rothschild Street, Rosebery, Sydney, NSW 2018, Australia

Printed in the United States of America by
Vicks Lithograph and Printing Corporation

Contents

BASIC SCALE THEORY

SCALE CONSTRUCTION

Scales are the foundation on which most music is based. A scale is made up of a series of tones arranged in a specific interval pattern. An *interval* is the distance between two tones, the smallest of which is called a *half step*. A half step corresponds to the closest distance between two piano keys.

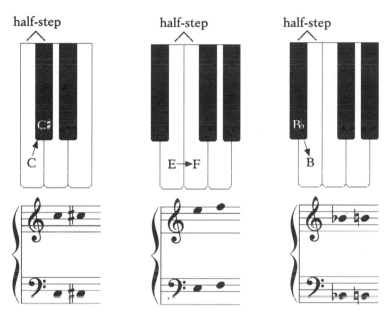

A *whole step* is equal to the distance of two half-steps. On the piano a whole step covers the distance of three keys.

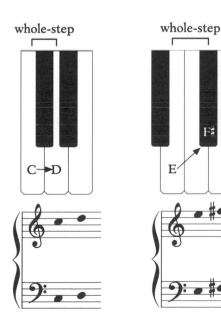
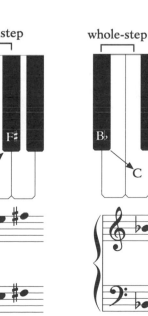

Half steps and whole steps are two basic types of *intervals* used when discussing the distance between neighboring notes in a scale. Other intervals are needed when talking about scale steps, or *degrees*, as they relate to each other or to the first tone, or *tonic*, of a scale. These intervals are named as follows.

Notice the minor second is the same as a half step and the major second is equal to a whole step.

MAJOR SCALES

The quality of a scale—whether it is major, minor, etc.—is determined by the arrangement of half steps and whole steps. The major scale has a half step between the third and fourth degrees and another between the seventh and eighth degrees. All other scale steps are separated from their neighbors by a whole step. This arrangement of half steps and whole steps is the same for all major scales.

C major scale

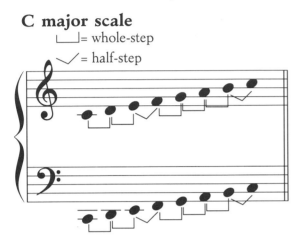

It is common to refer to scale steps by Roman numerals. Notice the relationship of these numbers to the naming of intervals.

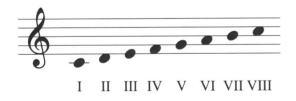

I   II   III   IV   V   VI   VII   VIII

KEY SIGNATURES

Now that you know how a C major scale is constructed, let's look at how this relates to other major scales. If you divide the C major scale in half, you will notice that the first half and second half each use the same configuration of half steps and whole steps—and that the two halves are separated by a whole step. Since the half-step/whole-step formula is the same for both halves of the scale, and since all major scales use the same formula, you can construct a new scale that begins with the second half of the C major scale. The example below shows that the resulting scale will be a G major scale. Unlike the C major scale, which has no sharps or flats, the G major scale must always have an F♯ to make it conform to the major-scale formula of half steps and whole steps. Since the key of G major always contains an F♯, this F♯ appears in the *key signature* of G major

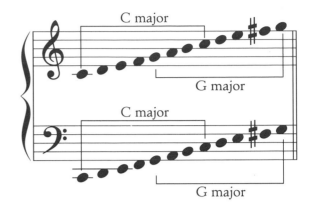

Key signature of G major

Now, do the same thing with a G major scale that we did above with the C scale. The new scale starts on D and has two sharps: F♯ and C♯. As a result, the key signature for D major contains two sharps. Notice that with each new scale the seventh degree is sharped and this sharp is added to the right of the previous sharps in the key signature.

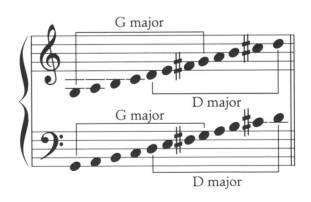

Key signature of D major

CIRCLE OF FIFTHS

By now you have probably noticed a pattern developing; we take the fifth degree of a scale to start a new scale, and with each new scale we add a sharp. The chart below is referred to as the *circle of fifths*— it starts with C major and progresses around the circle by fifths through all the keys, ending back at C major. By using this chart you will be able to play and write all twelve major scales.

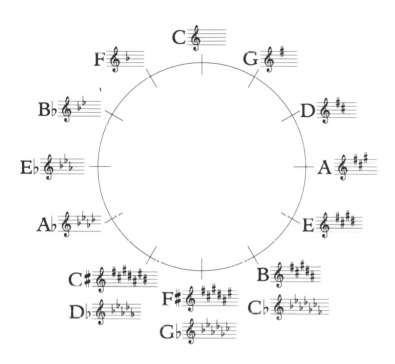

MINOR SCALES

There are three different types of minor scales: *natural, harmonic,* and *melodic.* All major scales have a corresponding *relative minor* scale. The scale can be found by starting on the sixth step of any major scale. For example, start on the sixth step of a C scale and by using the same formula for the major scale an A minor scale will created. Therefore, A minor is the relative minor of C major. This scale is said to be *natural,* or *pure,* because it follows the major-scale formula without altering the key signature.

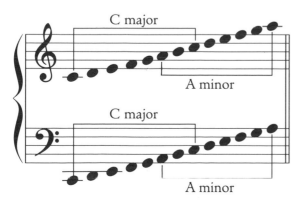

The harmonic minor scale has half steps between scale steps two and three, five and six, and seven and eight. Notice the distance between scale steps six and seven is a minor third.

A harmonic minor

The melodic minor scale's ascending order finds half steps between two and three and between seven and eight. Unlike any of the other scales that have been discussed so far, melodic minor scales have a different descending order. The descending order has half steps between degrees six and five and between three and two—with a whole step between steps eight and seven.

A melodic minor ascending

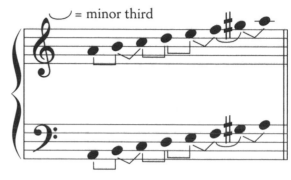

A melodic minor descending

How to Use This Book

The subsequent pages are a graphic and musical representation of the major, harmonic minor, and melodic minor scales, and the Dorian, Phrygian, Lydian, Mixolydian, Aeolian, and Locrian modes.

Each scale is displayed as a diagram and in music notation. The scales in each section start with no sharps and no flats and continue in order through the "circle of fifths" (see page 7) until all twelve scales are demonstrated.

The keyboard diagram consists of two elements, the notes to be played in the scale and the fingering to be used. The gray keys on the keyboard diagram show which notes are to be played.

The white circles with numbers inside them represent the right-hand fingering and the black circles are for the left-hand fingering. The numbers inside the circles

correspond to the fingers of each hand with ① being the thumb, ② the index finger, ③ the forefinger, ④ the ring finger, and ⑤ the pinky finger.

Below the keyboard diagram is the scale written in music notation. To the right of the clefs in the treble and bass are the key signatures (see page 6), to the right of them are notes of the scale. The small numbers that appear over some of the notes are fingering numbers. Notice that only certain notes are numbered, the first and last notes and the *pivot points*. Pivot points are where the fingers cross over the thumb or the thumb crosses under the fingers.

The keyboard diagram and music display the fingering and notation for two octaves of the scale. It is good practice to play and learn both octaves, this will improve your reading skills and dexterity.

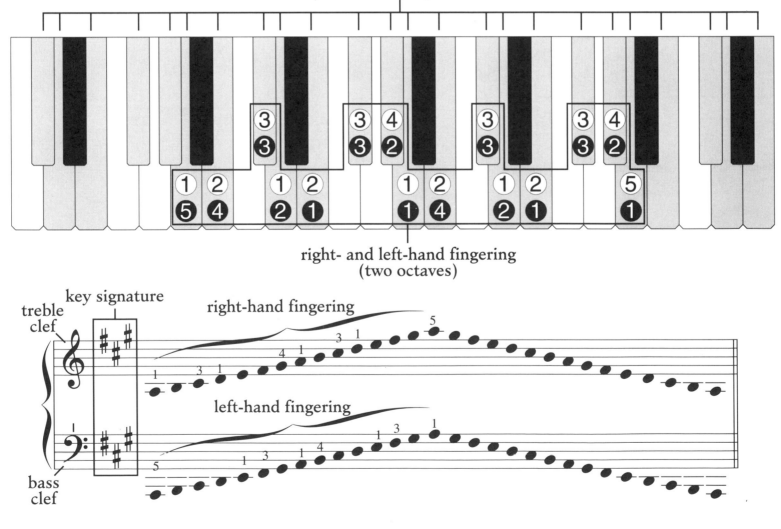

keys that make up the scale

right- and left-hand fingering
(two octaves)

treble clef — key signature — right-hand fingering — left-hand fingering — bass clef

C MAJOR

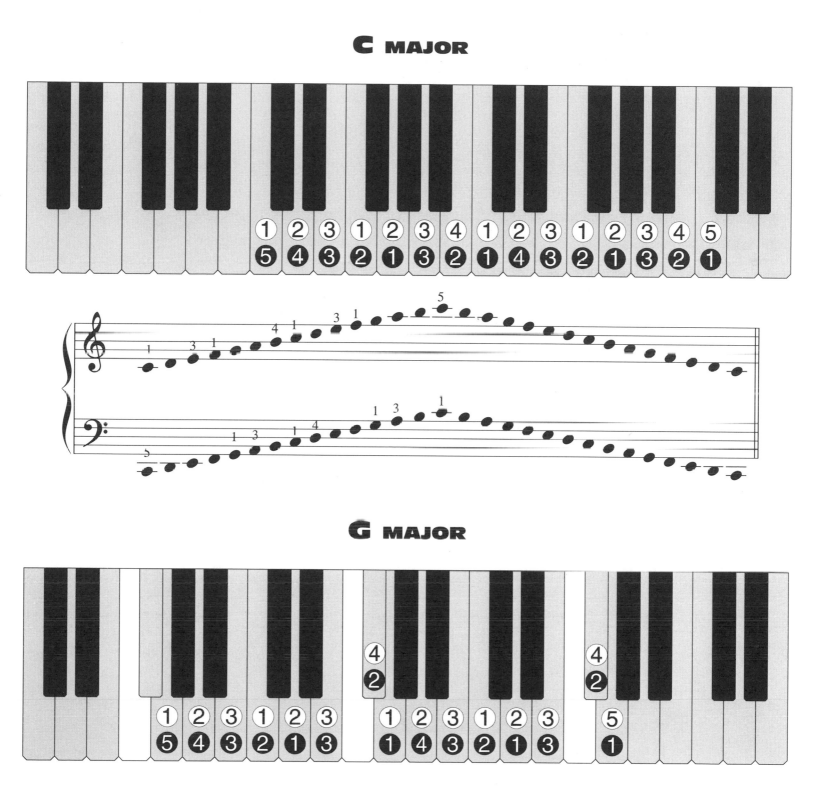

G MAJOR

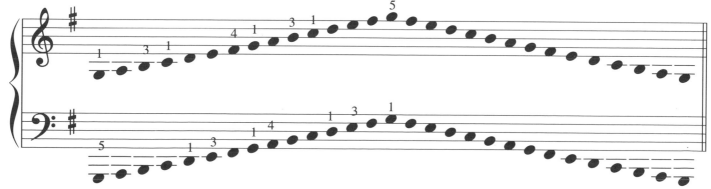

D MAJOR

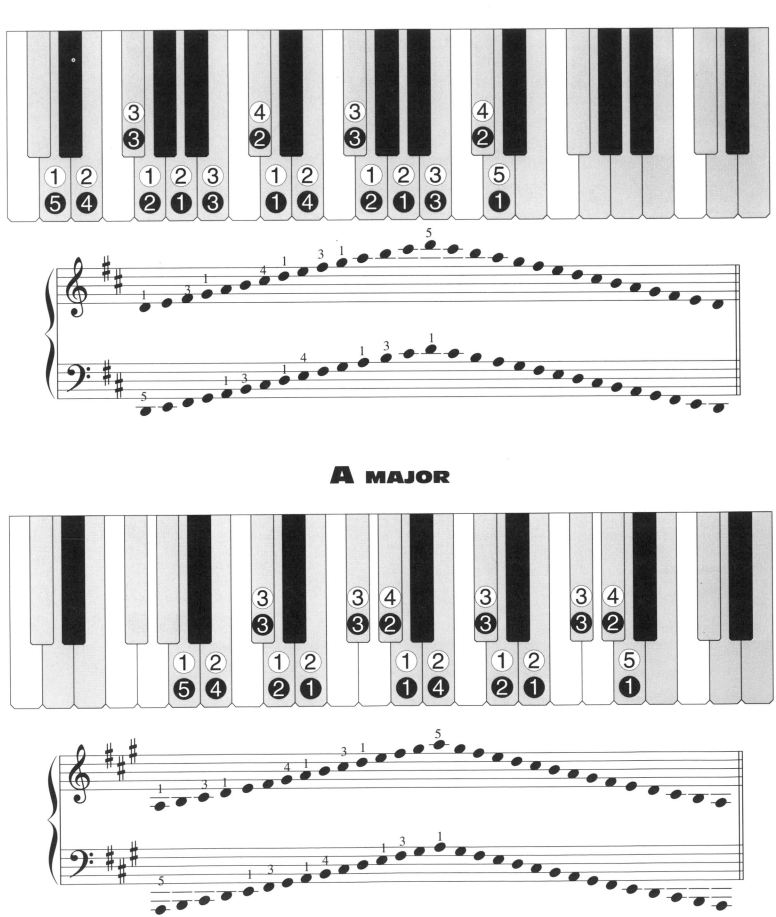

A MAJOR

E MAJOR

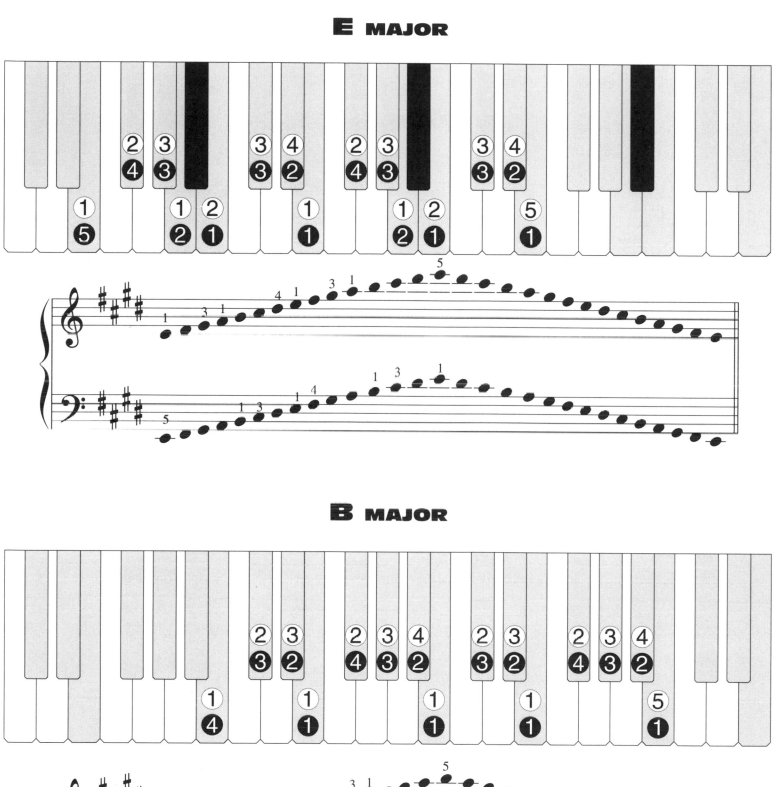

B MAJOR

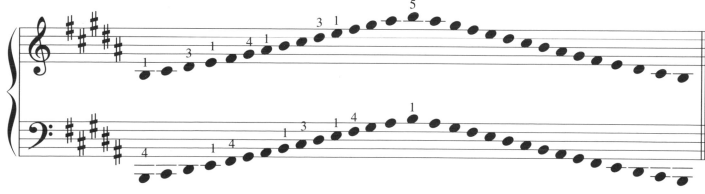

F# MAJOR

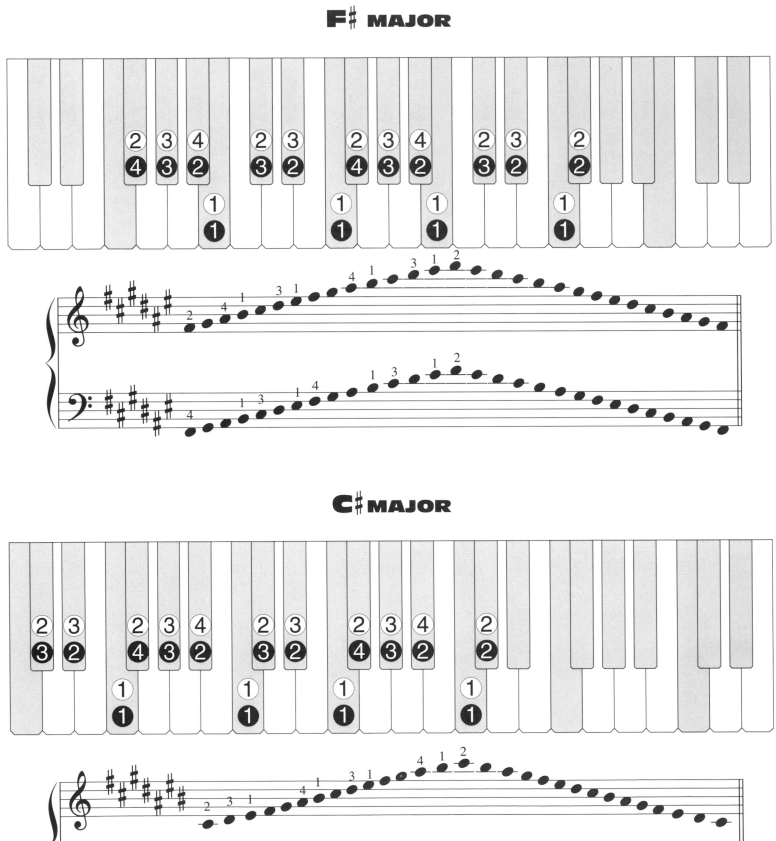

C# MAJOR

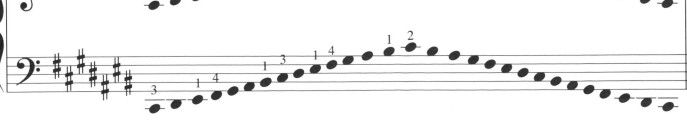

F MAJOR

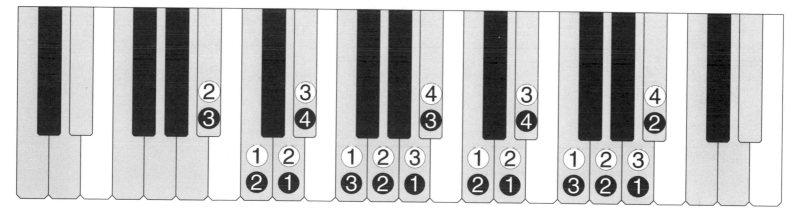

B♭ MAJOR

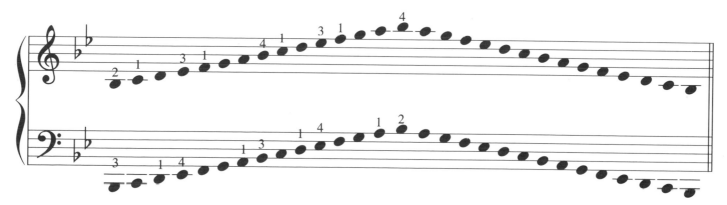

E♭ MAJOR

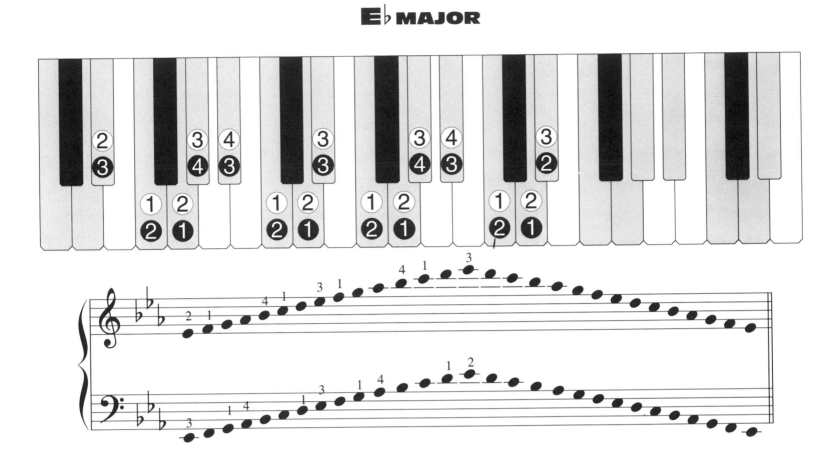

A♭ MAJOR

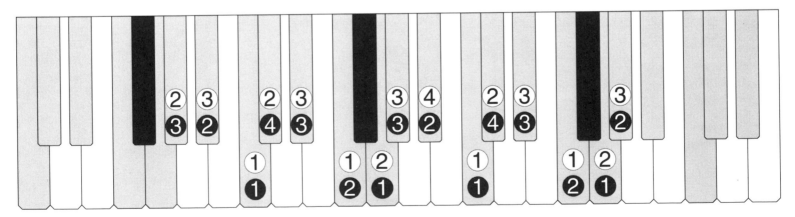

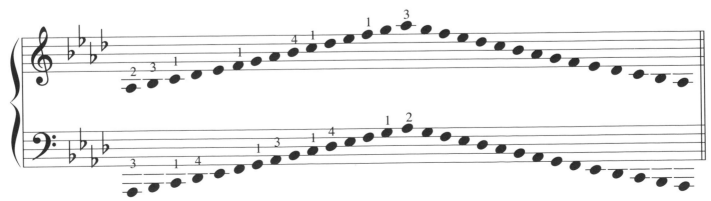

D♭ MAJOR

G♭ MAJOR

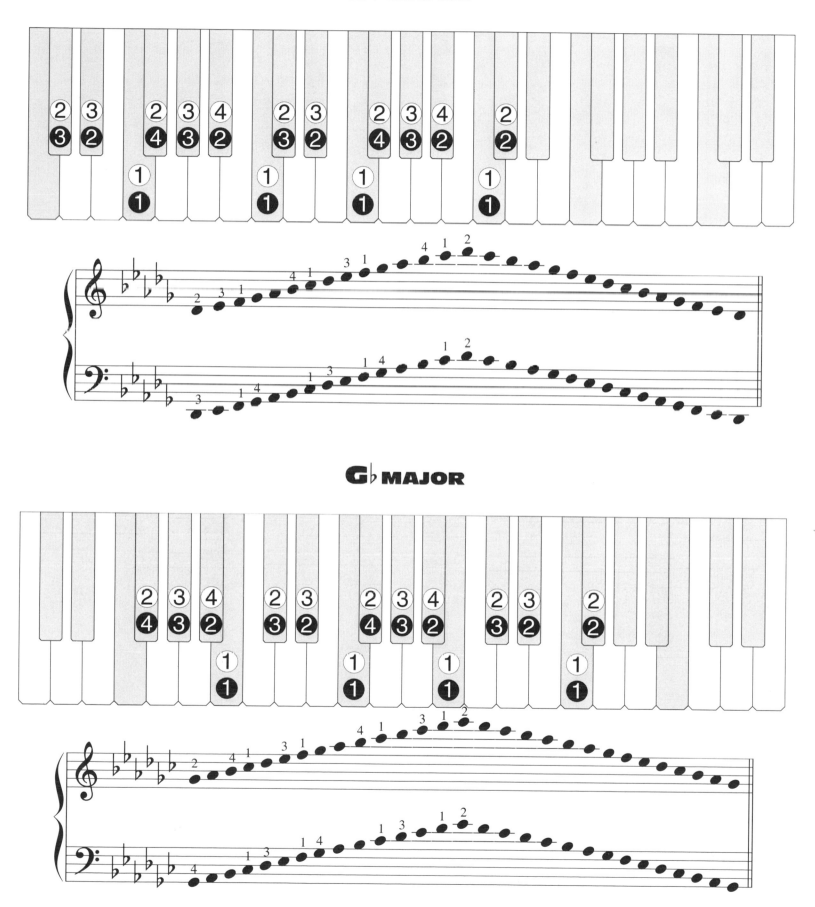

C♭ MAJOR

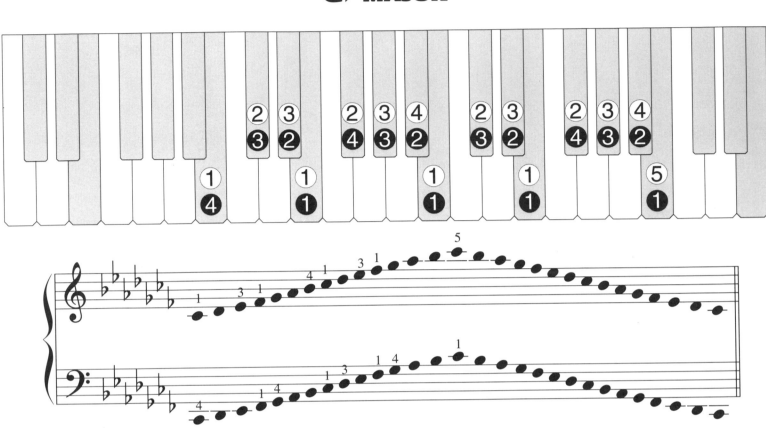

A HARMONIC MINOR

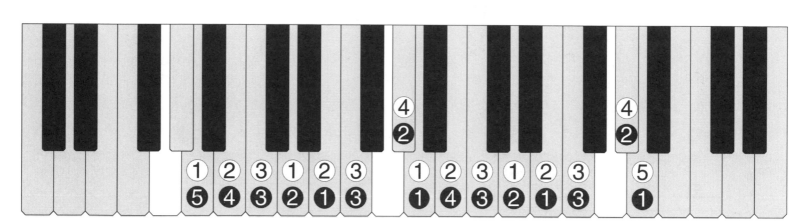

E HARMONIC MINOR

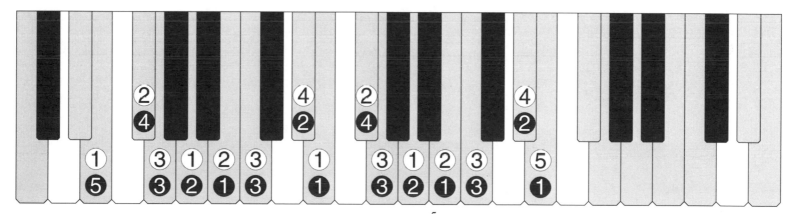

B HARMONIC MINOR

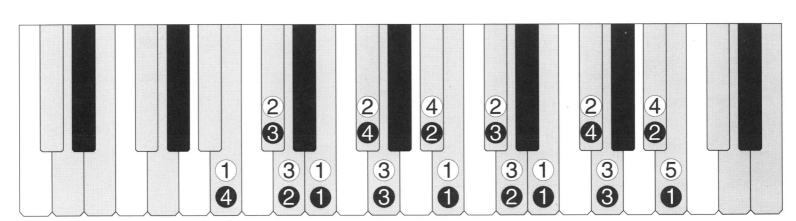

F# HARMONIC MINOR

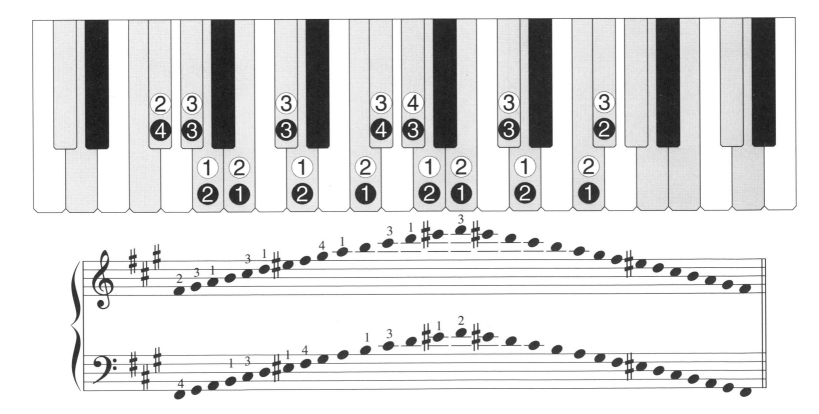

C# HARMONIC MINOR

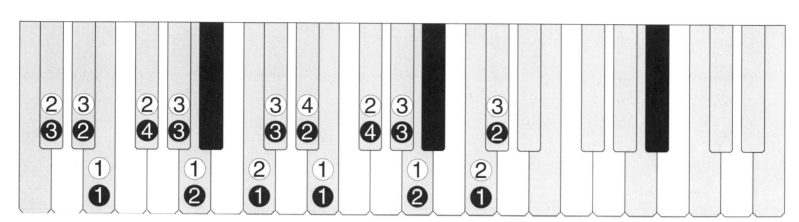

G# HARMONIC MINOR

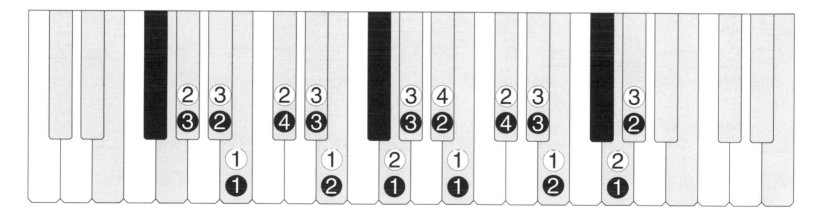

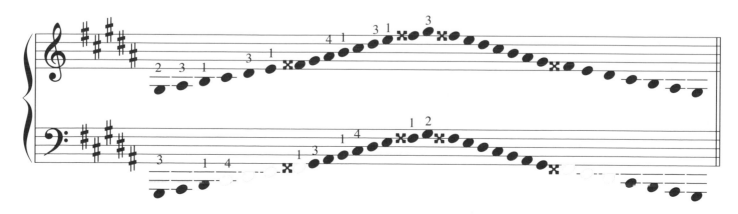

D♯ HARMONIC MINOR

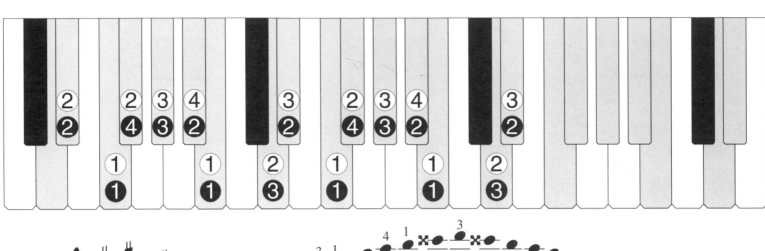

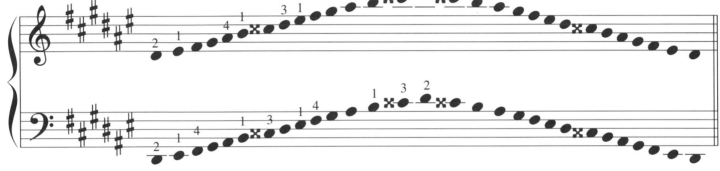

A♯ HARMONIC MINOR

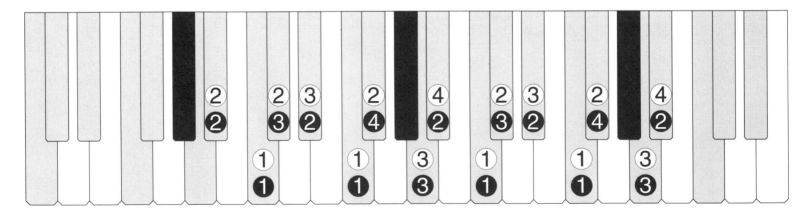

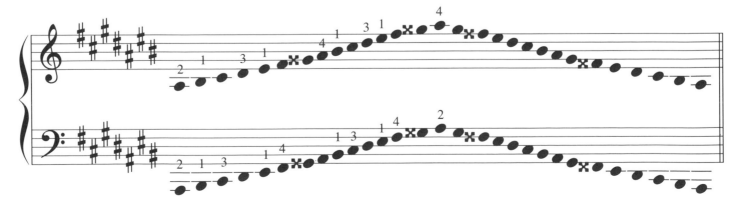

D HARMONIC MINOR

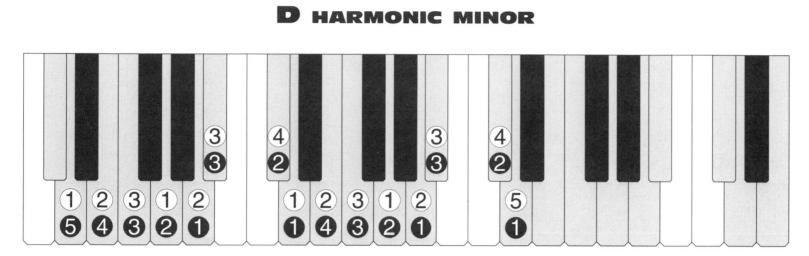

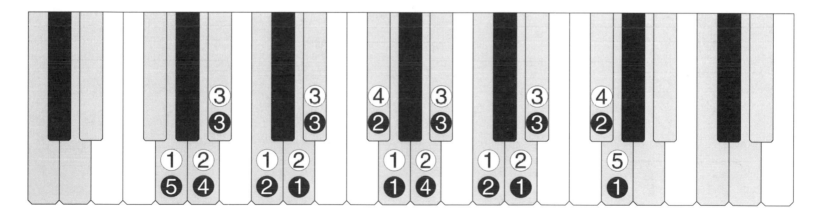

G HARMONIC MINOR

C harmonic minor

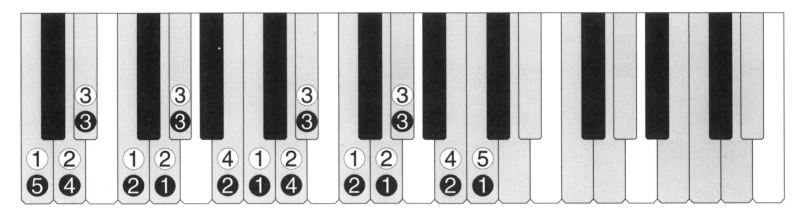

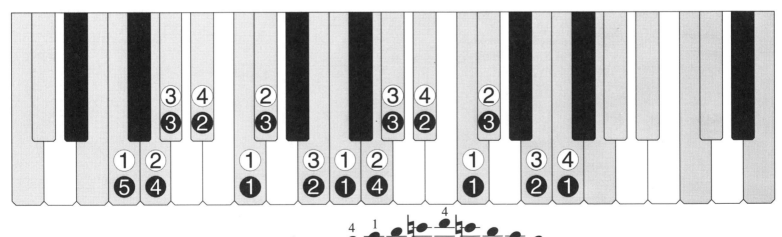

F harmonic minor

B♭ HARMONIC MINOR

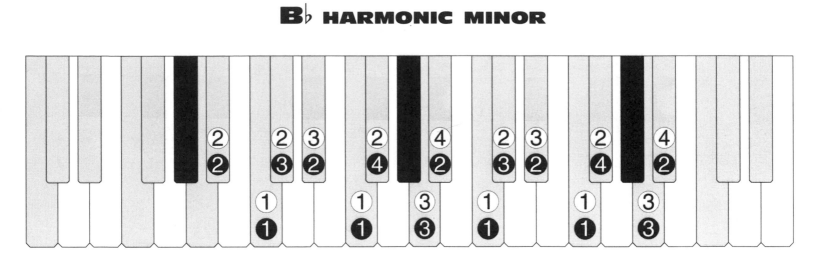

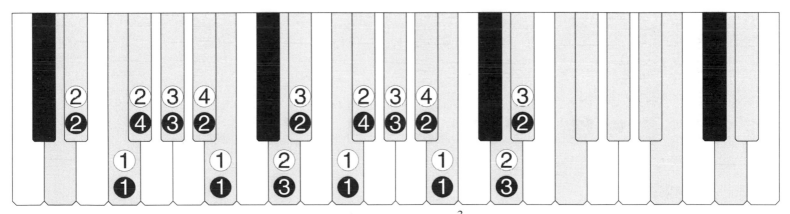

E♭ HARMONIC MINOR

A♭ Harmonic Minor

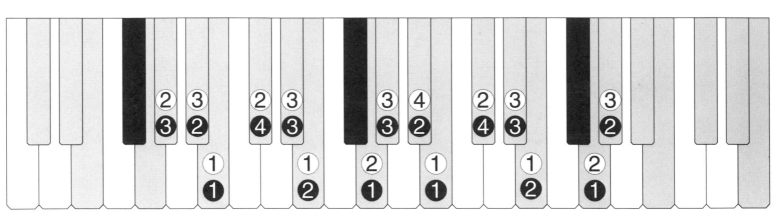

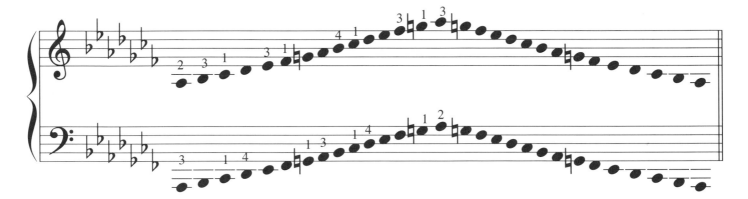

A MELODIC MINOR
ascending

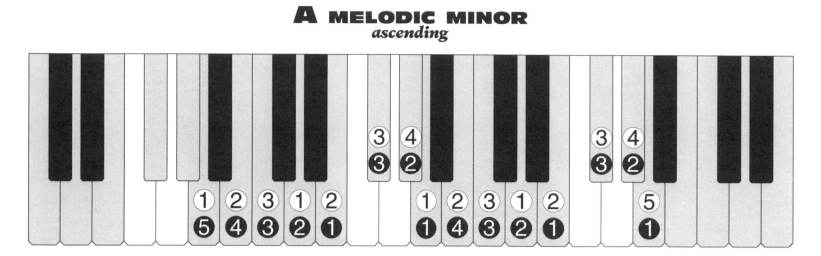

A MELODIC MINOR
descending

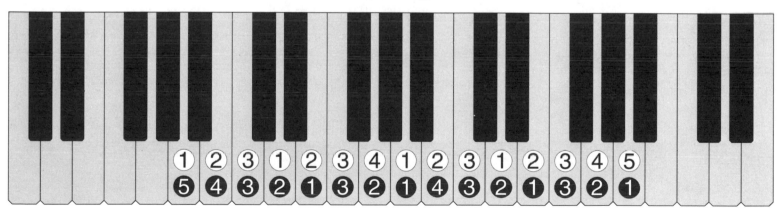

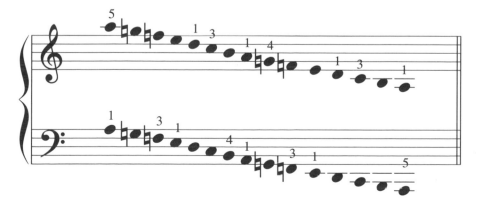

E MELODIC MINOR
ascending

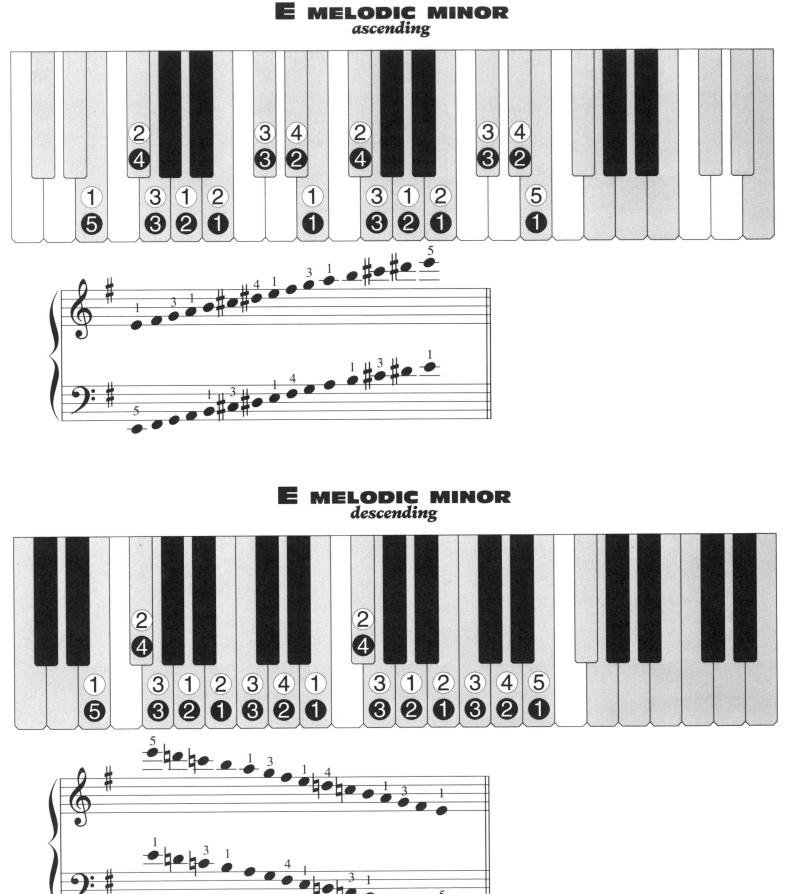

E MELODIC MINOR
descending

B MELODIC MINOR
ascending

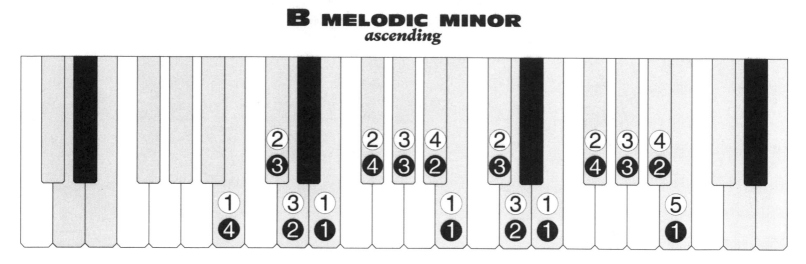

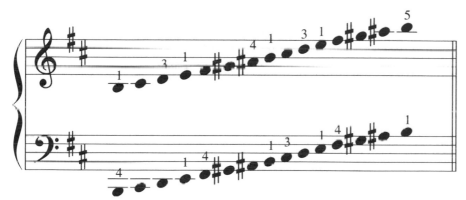

B MELODIC MINOR
descending

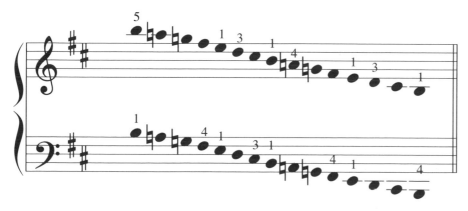

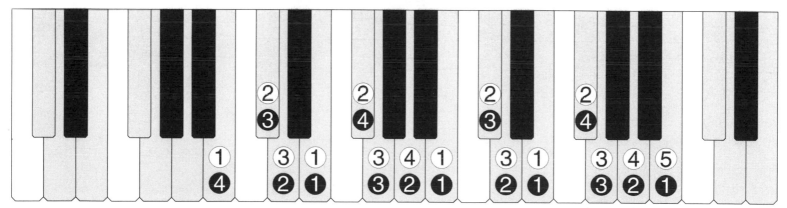

F♯ MELODIC MINOR
ascending

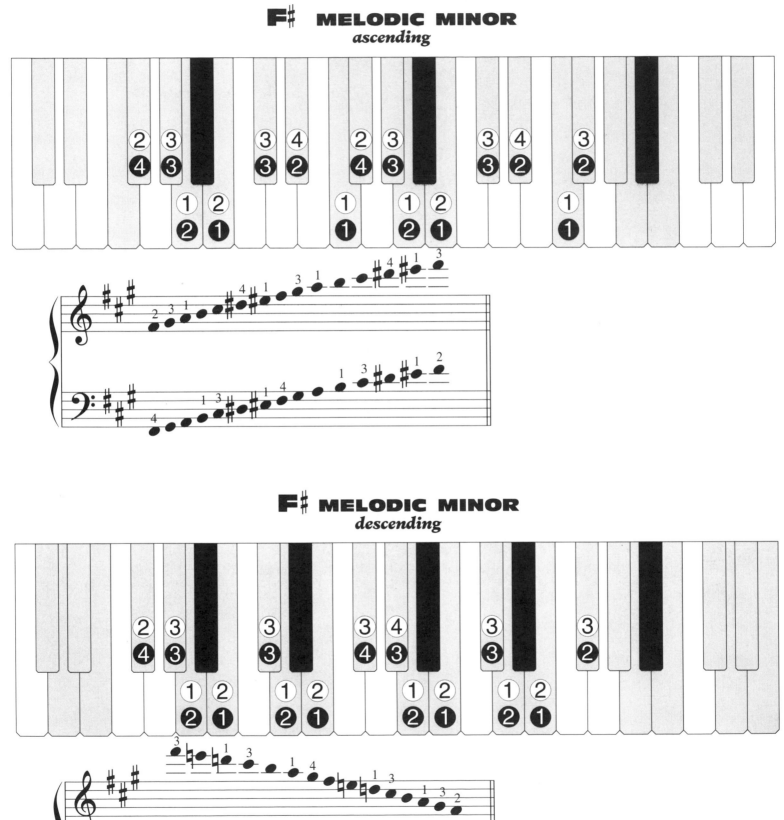

F♯ MELODIC MINOR
descending

C# MELODIC MINOR
ascending

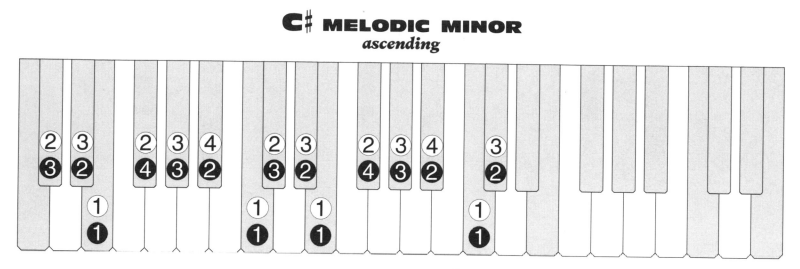

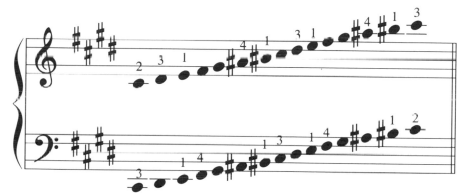

C# MELODIC MINOR
descending

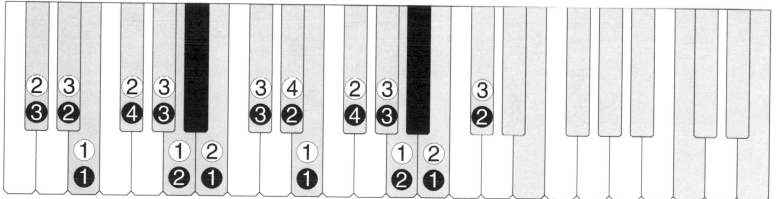

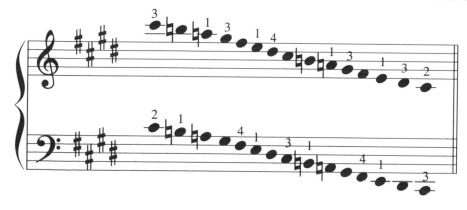

G♯ MELODIC MINOR
ascending

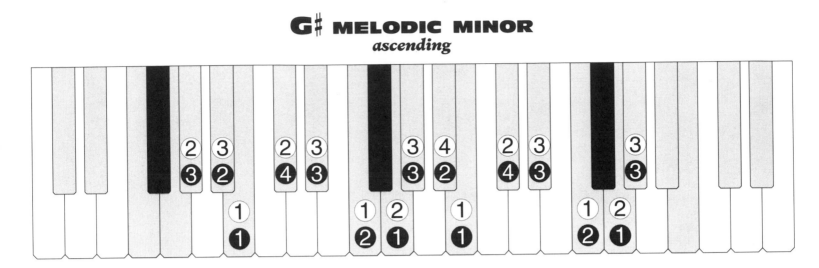

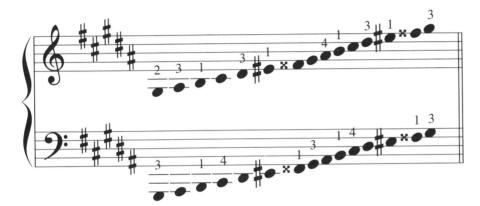

G♯ MELODIC MINOR
descending

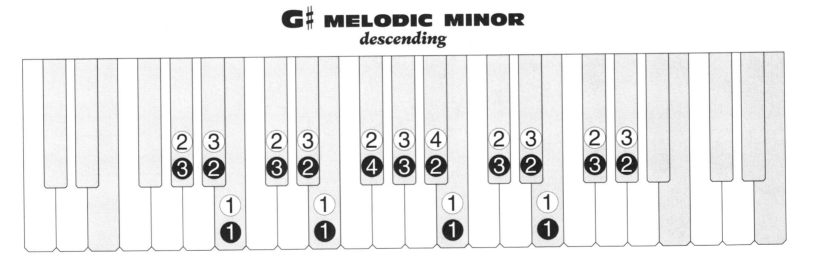

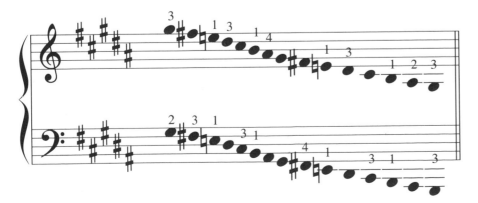

D♯ MELODIC MINOR
ascending

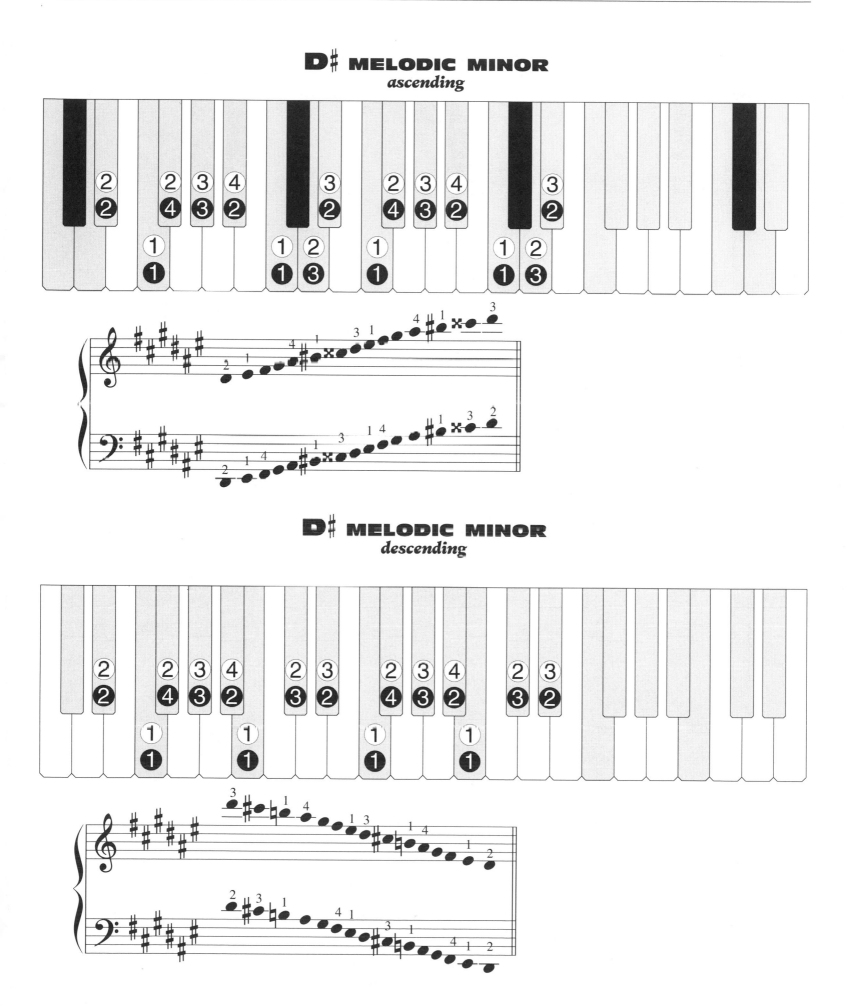

D♯ MELODIC MINOR
descending

A♯ MELODIC MINOR
ascending

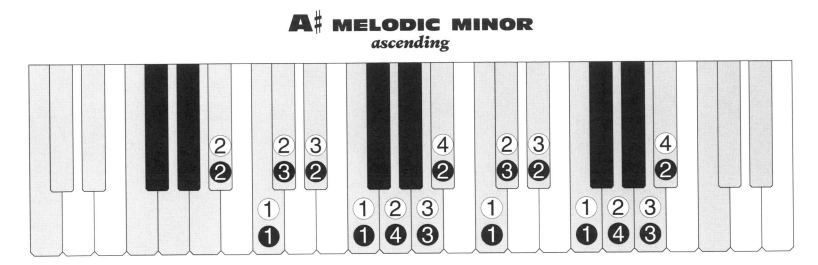

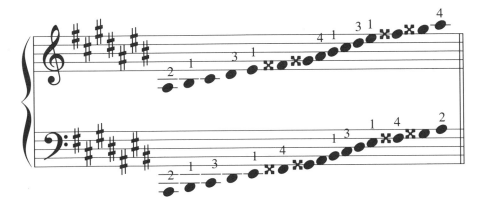

A♯ MELODIC MINOR
descending

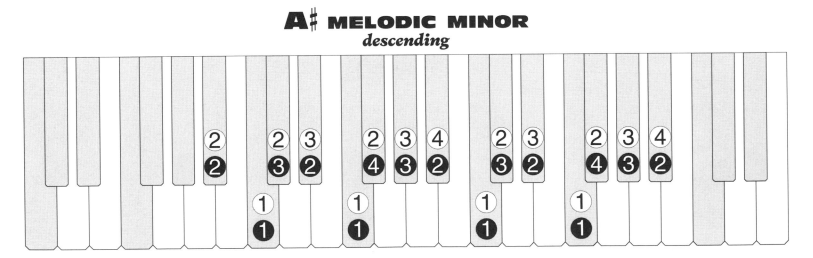

D MELODIC MINOR
ascending

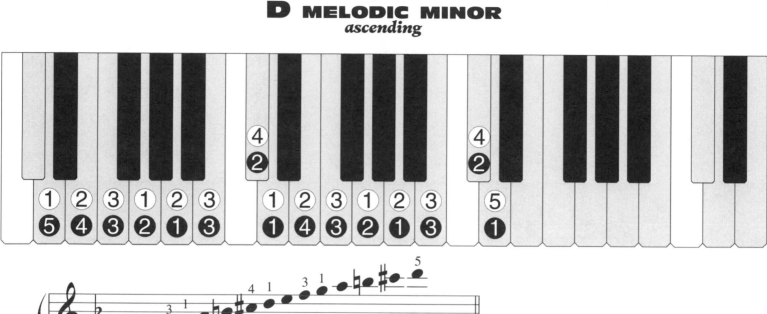

D MELODIC MINOR
descending

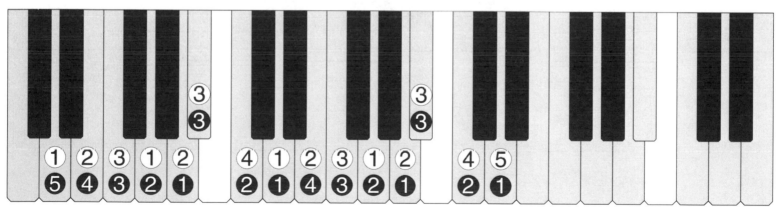

G MELODIC MINOR
ascending

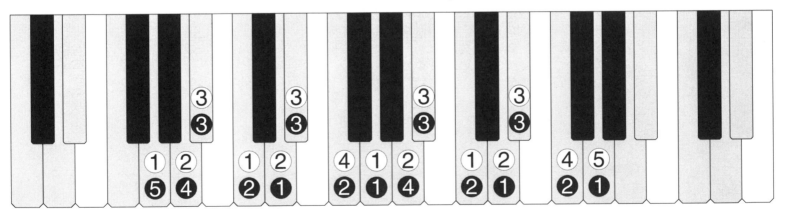

G MELODIC MINOR
descending

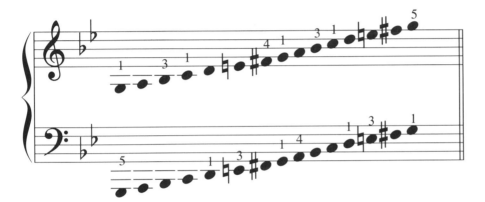

C MELODIC MINOR
ascending

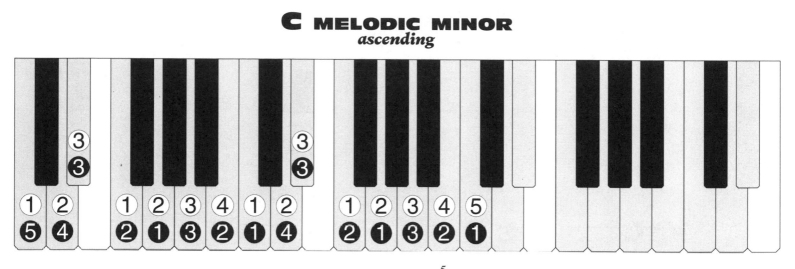

C MELODIC MINOR
descending

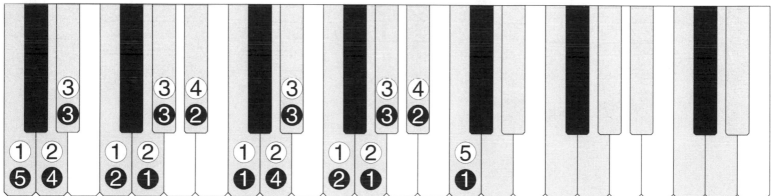

F MELODIC MINOR
ascending

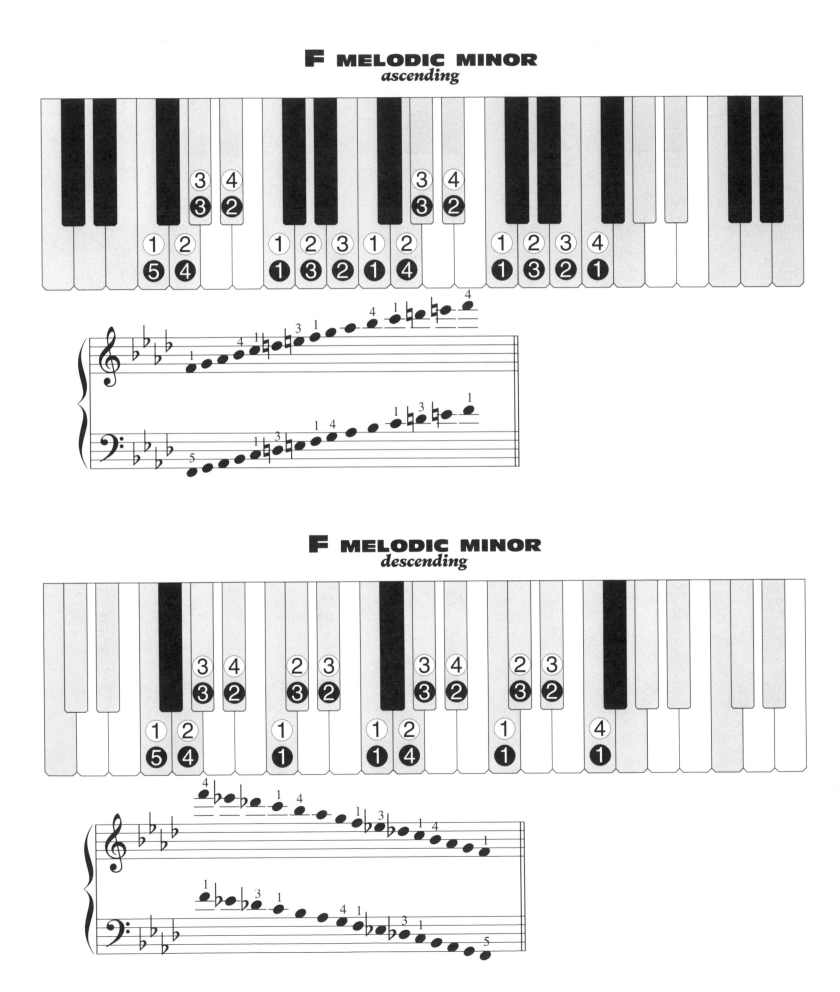

F MELODIC MINOR
descending

B♭ MELODIC MINOR
ascending

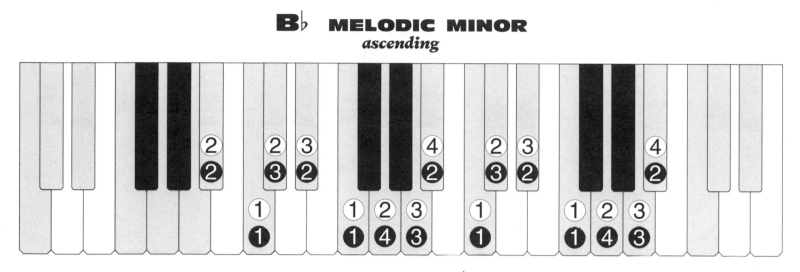

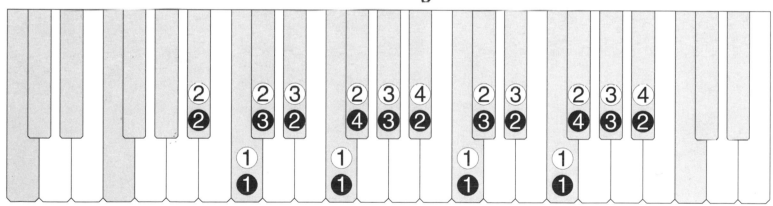

B♭ MELODIC MINOR
descending

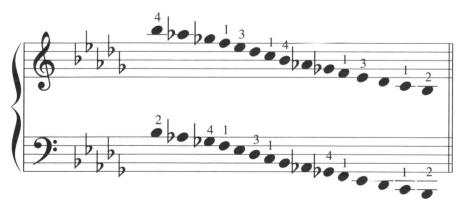

E♭ MELODIC MINOR
ascending

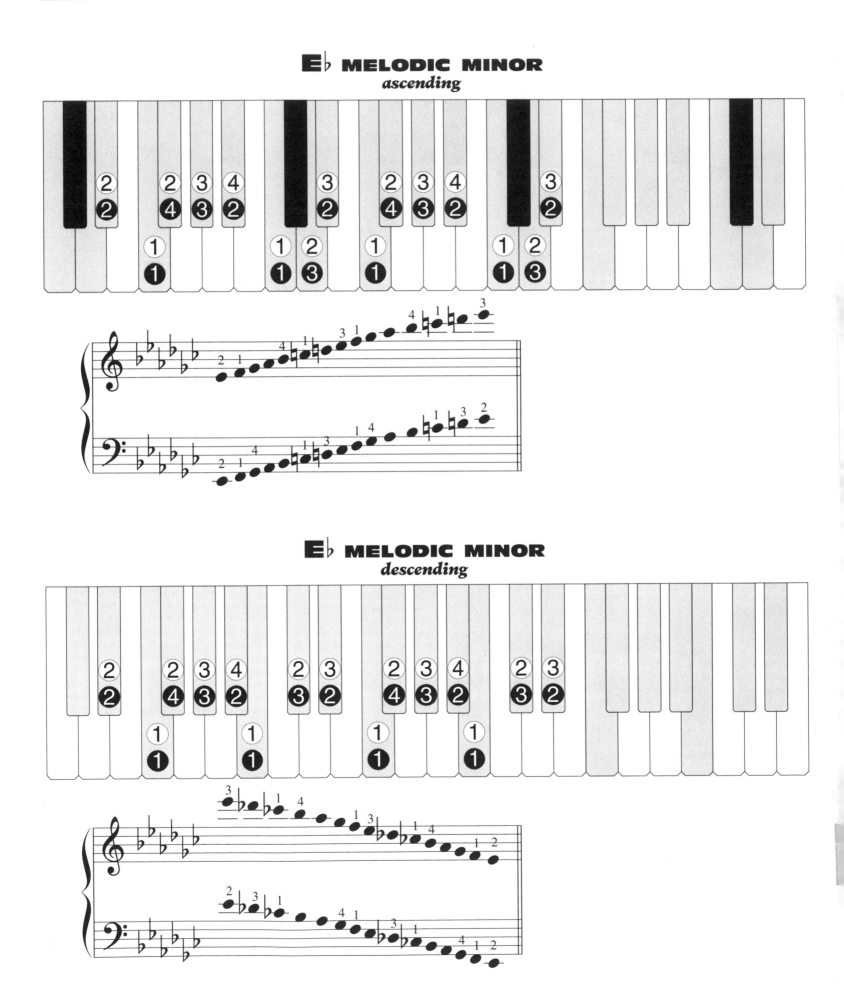

E♭ MELODIC MINOR
descending

A♭ MELODIC MINOR
ascending

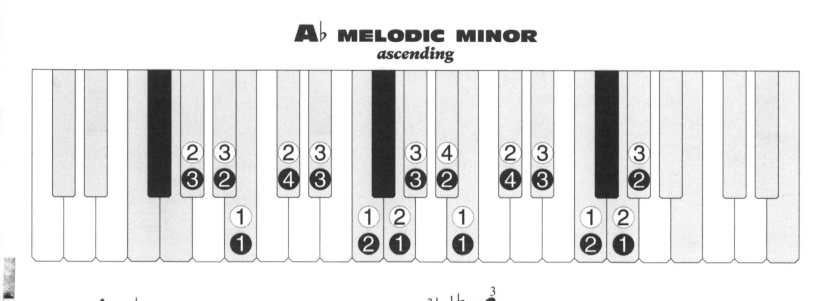

A♭ MELODIC MINOR
descending

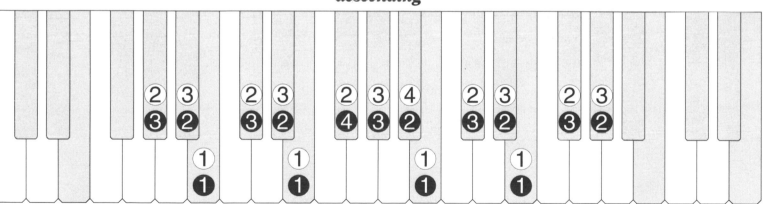

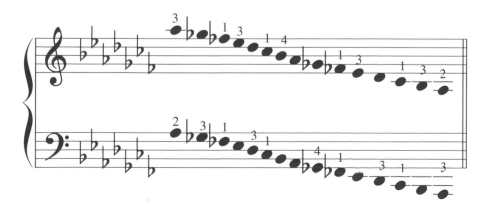

DORIAN

The Dorian scale begins on the second degree of the major scale. The half steps in the scale occur between degrees two and three, and six and seven. The Dorian scale resembles the natural minor scale with a sharped sixth.

D Dorian scale

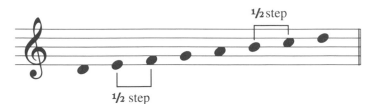

You can find this mode in many twentieth century, jazz, and jazz rock pieces. It is very useful when soloing over minor seventh chords.

Here are the basic triads of the Dorian scale, with major, minor, and diminished chords.

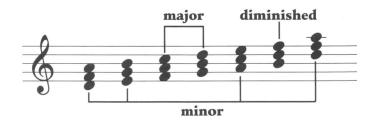

The following is a list of musical works which use the Dorian mode:
Pelléas et Mélisande by Claude Debussy
Concerto Gregoriano by Ottorino Respighi
Socrate by Erik Satie
Black Magic Woman by Carlos Santana
Oye Como Va by Santana
Greensleeves

D DORIAN

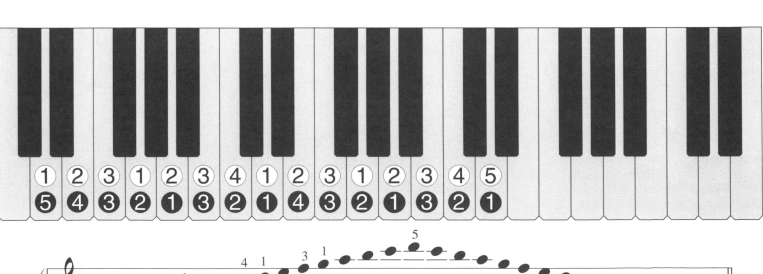

A DORIAN

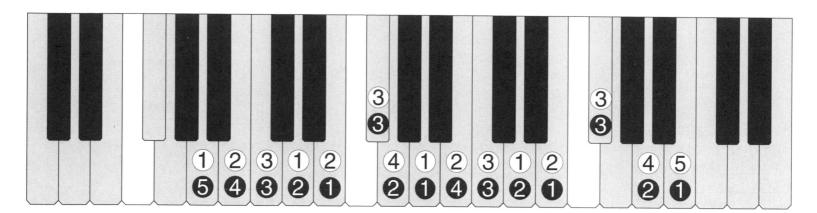

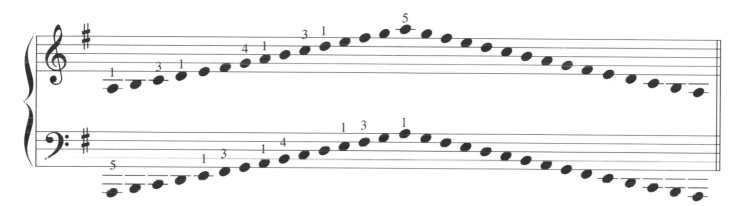

E DORIAN

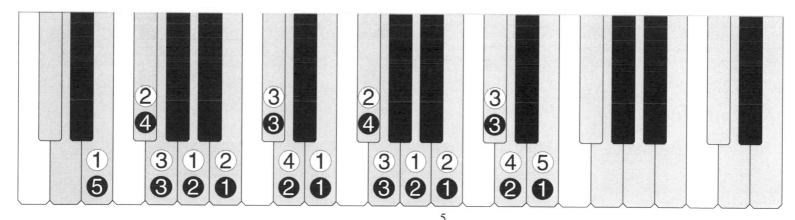

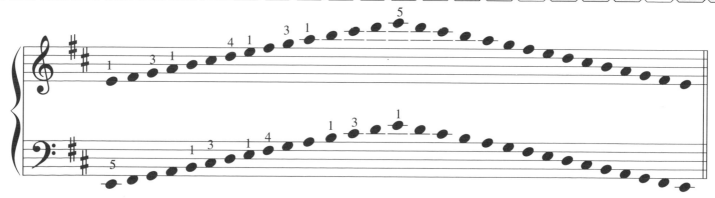

B Dorian

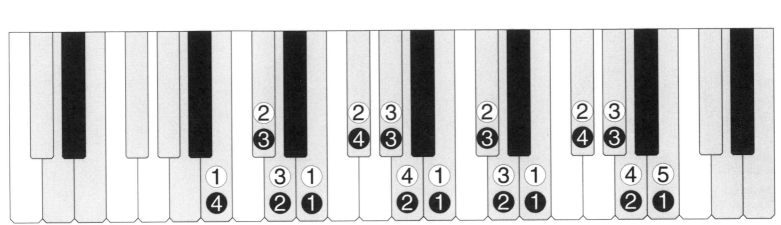

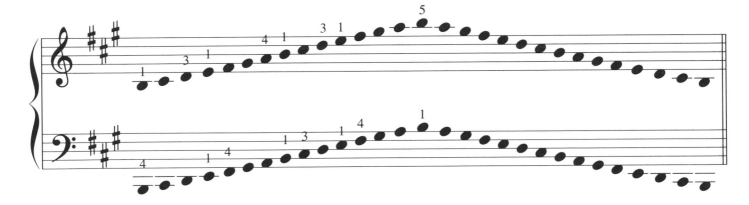

F♯ Dorian

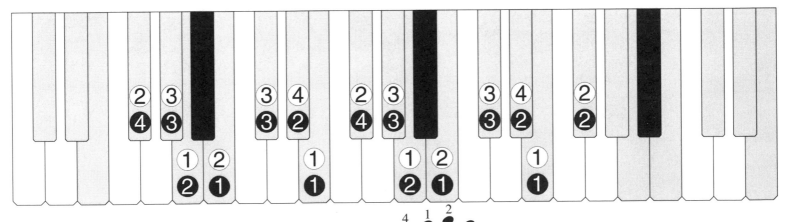

C# DORIAN

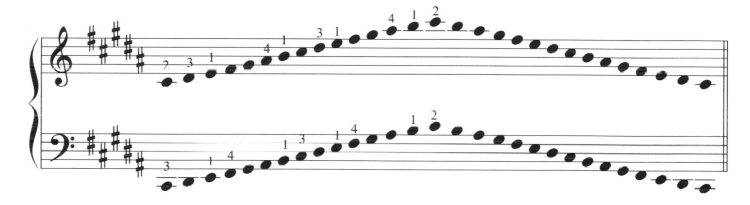

G# DORIAN

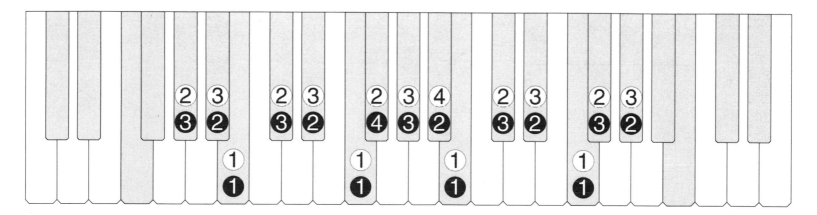

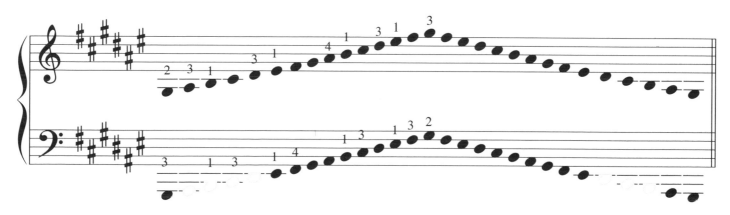

D♯ Dorian

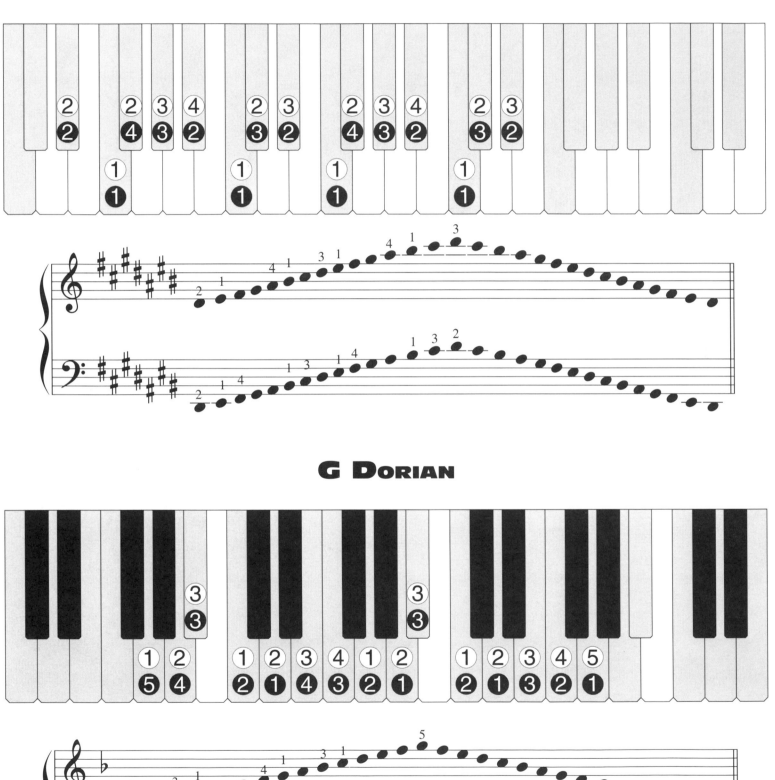

G Dorian

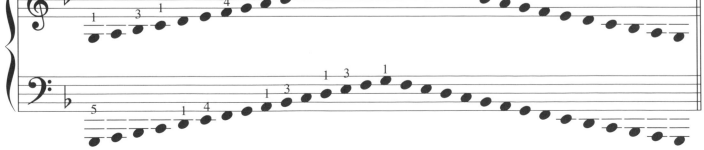

C DORIAN

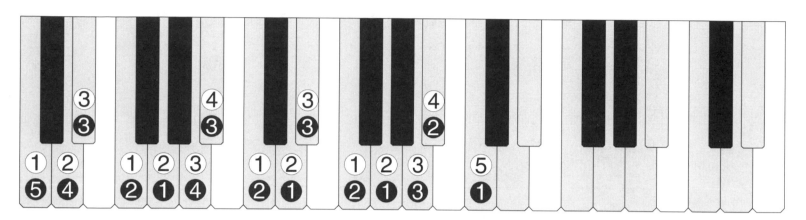

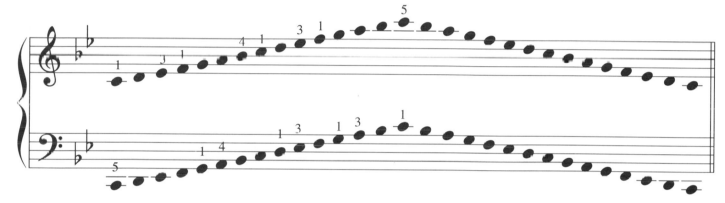

F DORIAN

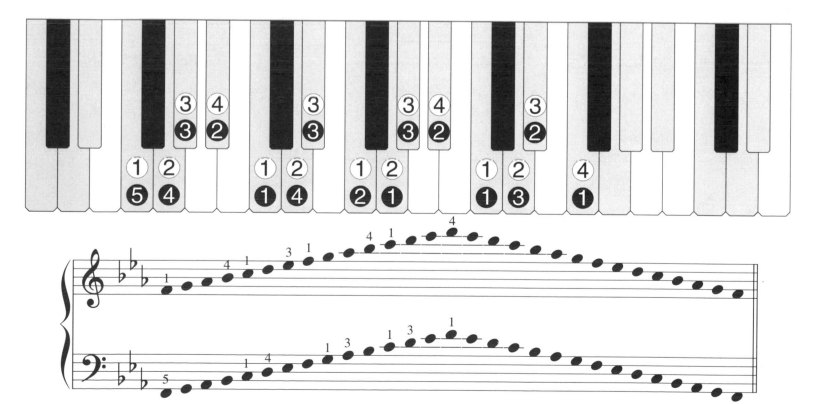

B♭ Dorian

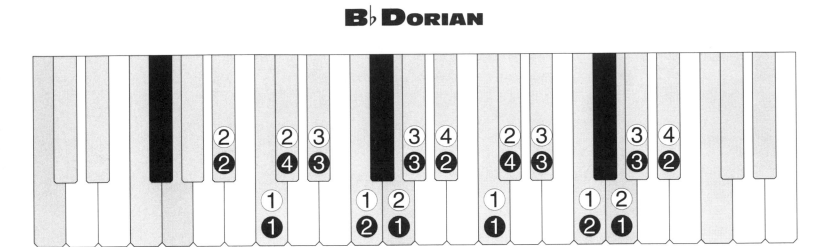

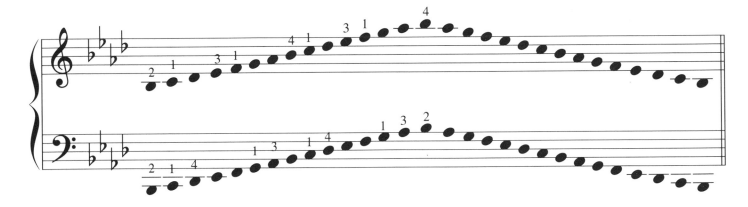

E♭ Dorian

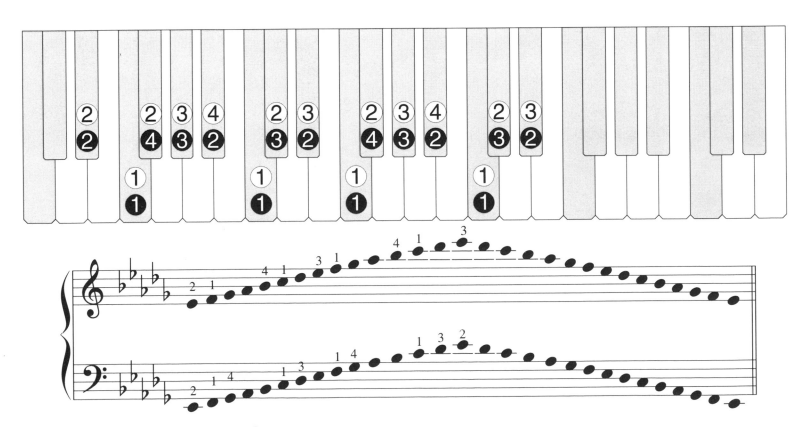

Ab DORIAN

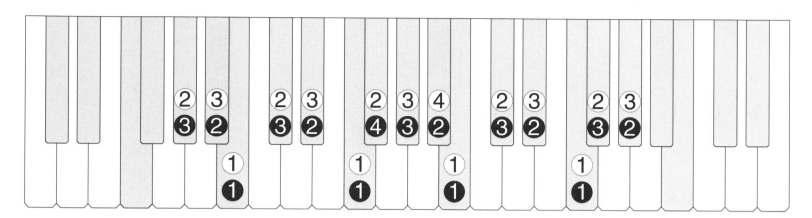

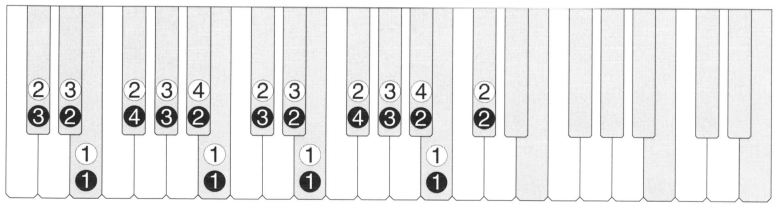

Db DORIAN

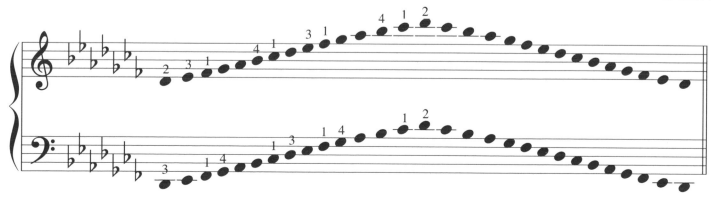

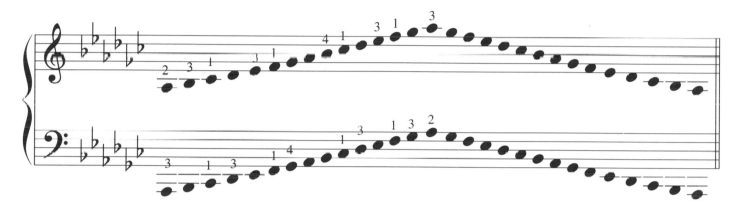

PHRYGIAN

The Phrygian scale begins on the third degree of the major scale. The Phrygian scale features half steps between degrees one and two, and five and six.

E Phrygian scale

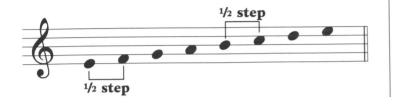

The Phrygian scale resembles the natural minor scale with a flatted second and has a distinctive flamenco or Spanish flavor.

Here are the basic triads of the Phrygian scale, with major, minor, and diminished chords indicated.

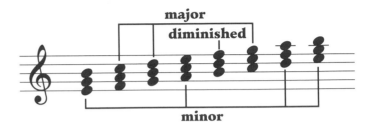

These musical works make significant use of the Phrygian mode:
String Quartet by Claude Debussy
Piano Preludes by Carlos Chávez
Symphony # 5 by Dmitri Shostakovich
Bungalow Bill (guitar intro) by Lennon & McCartney
Need Song by Yngwie Malmsteen

E PHRYGIAN

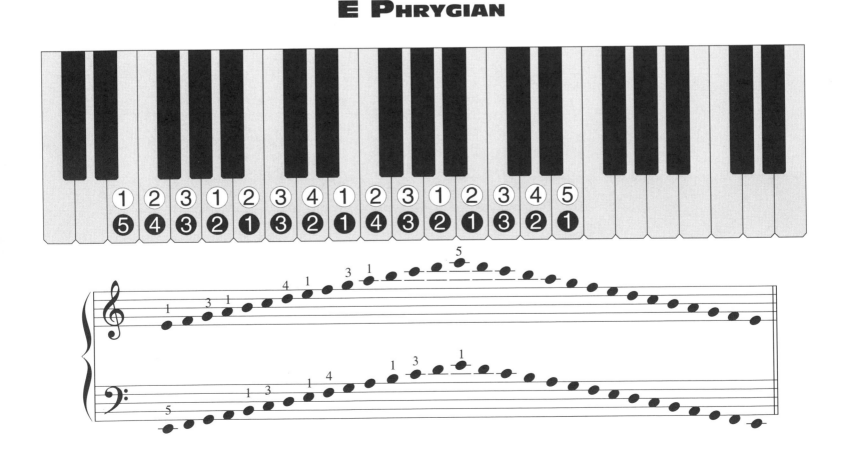

B PHRYGIAN

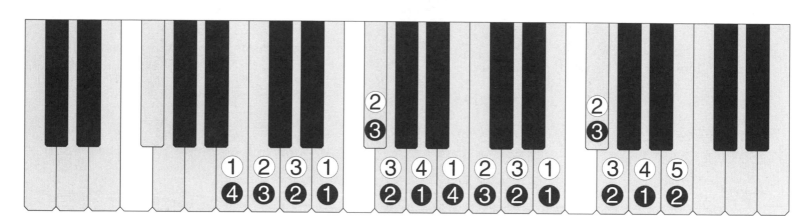

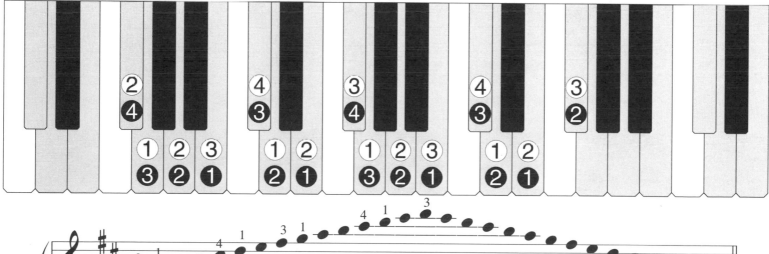

F♯ PHRYGIAN

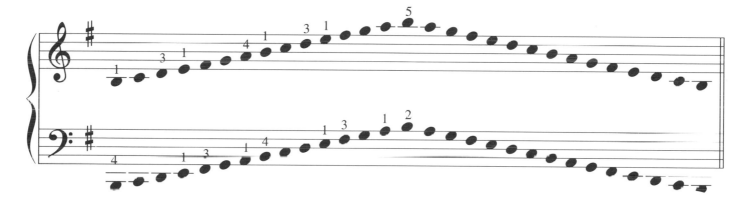

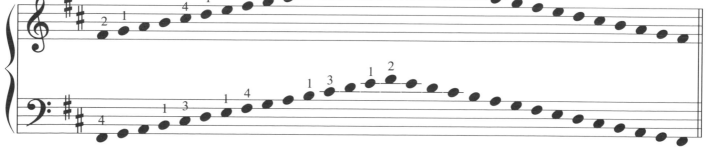

C# Phrygian

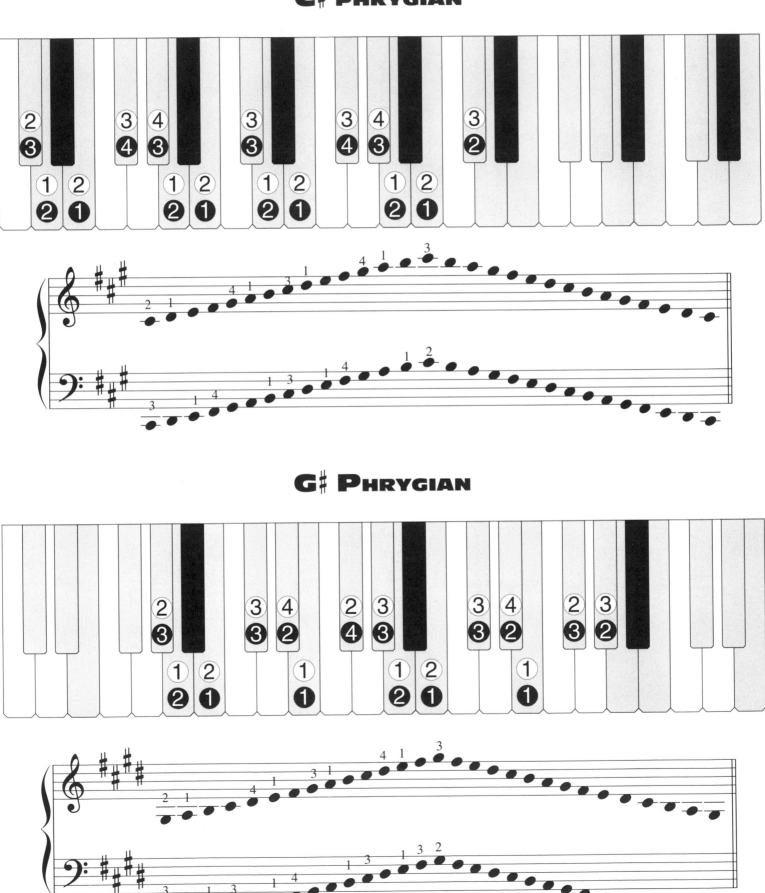

G# Phrygian

D♯ PHRYGIAN

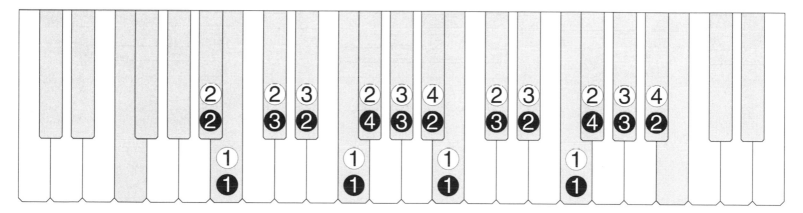

A♯ PHRYGIAN

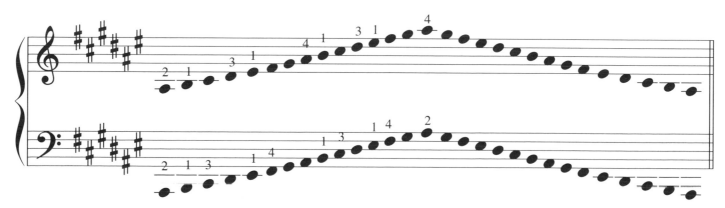

E♯ Phrygian

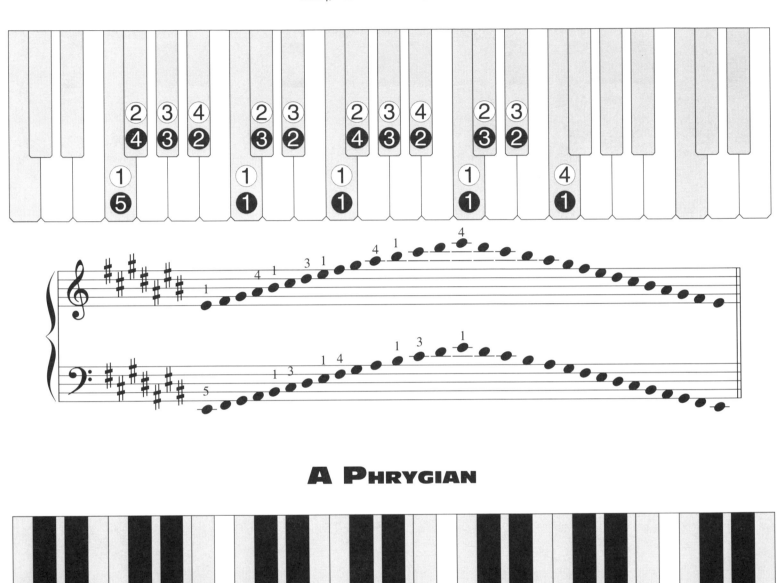

A Phrygian

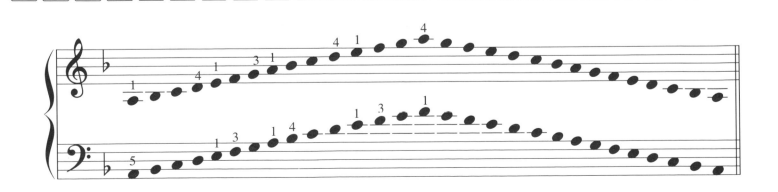

D PHRYGIAN

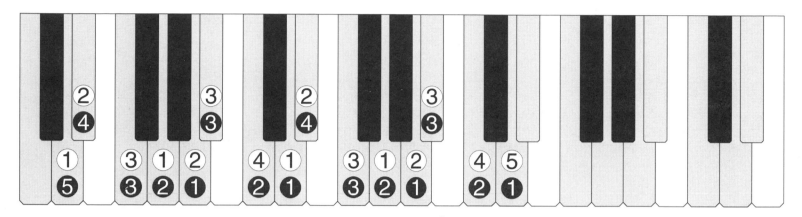

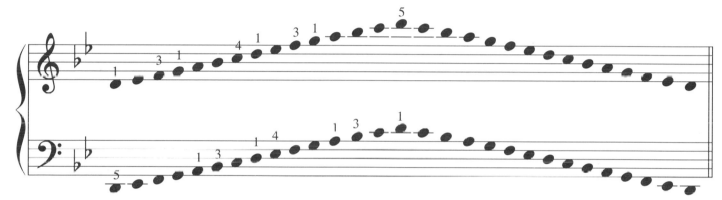

G PHRYGIAN

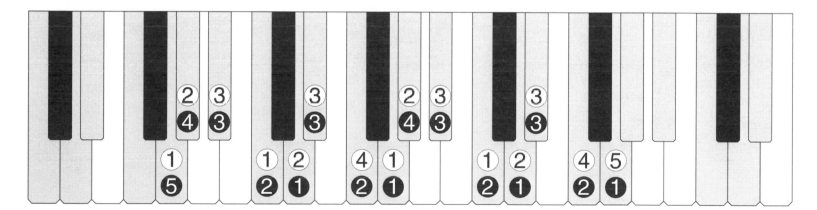

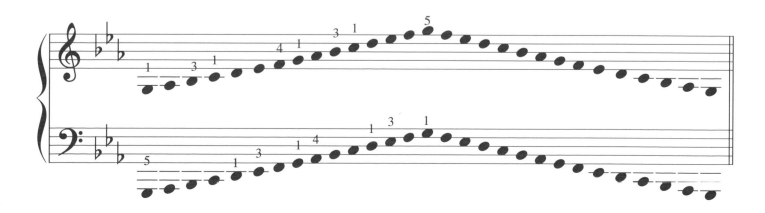

C Phrygian

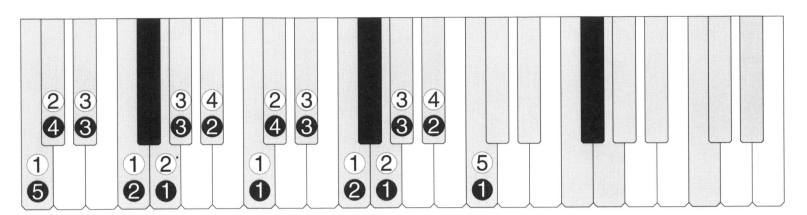

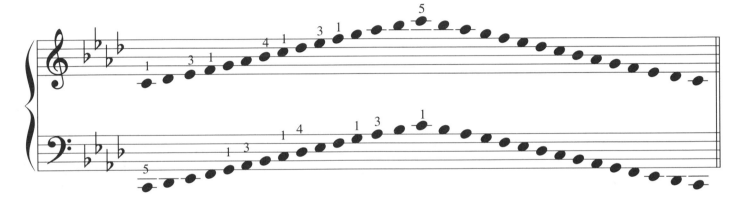

F Phrygian

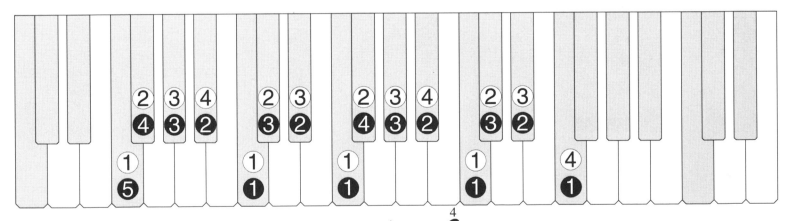

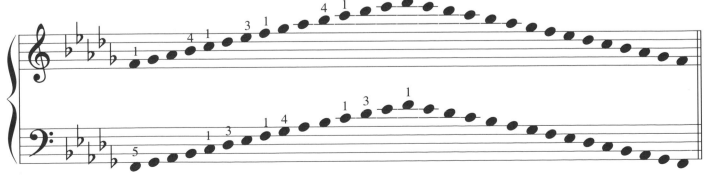

B♭ PHRYGIAN

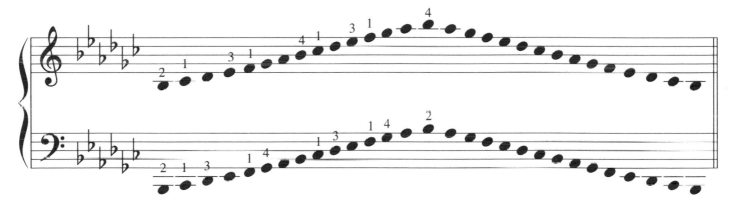

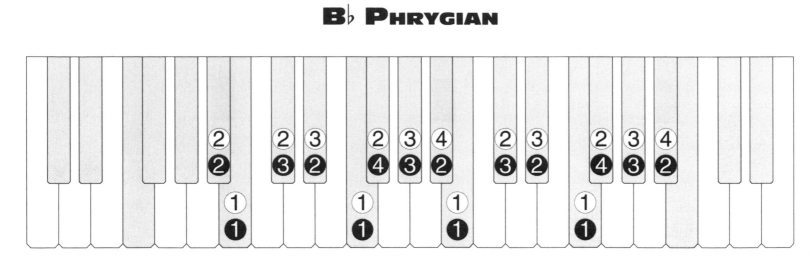

E♭ PHRYGIAN

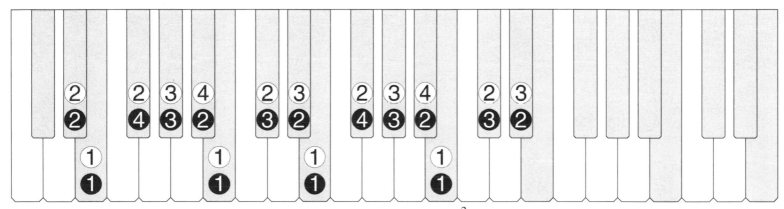

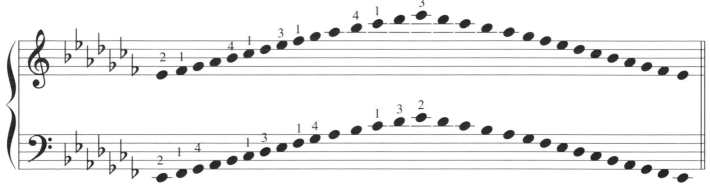

LYDIAN

The Lydian scale begins on the fourth degree of the major scale. The half steps of the Lydian scale occur between degrees four and five, and seven and eight.

F Lydian scale

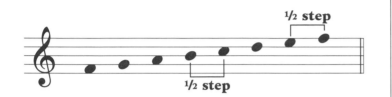

The Lydian scale has a major sound, but unlike the major scale, the fourth is raised. Lydian scales are useful in jazz when playing over major seventh chords (with the exception of the I chord).

Here are the basic triads of the Lydian scale, with major, minor, and diminished chords indicated.

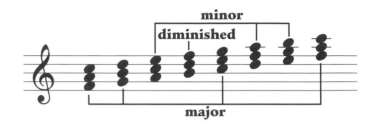

These musical works make significant use of the Lydian mode:
Trois Chansons by Maurice Ravel
Protée by Darius Milhaud
Seven Sonnets of Michalangelo by Benjamin Britten
Flying in a Blue Dream by Joe Satriani

F LYDIAN

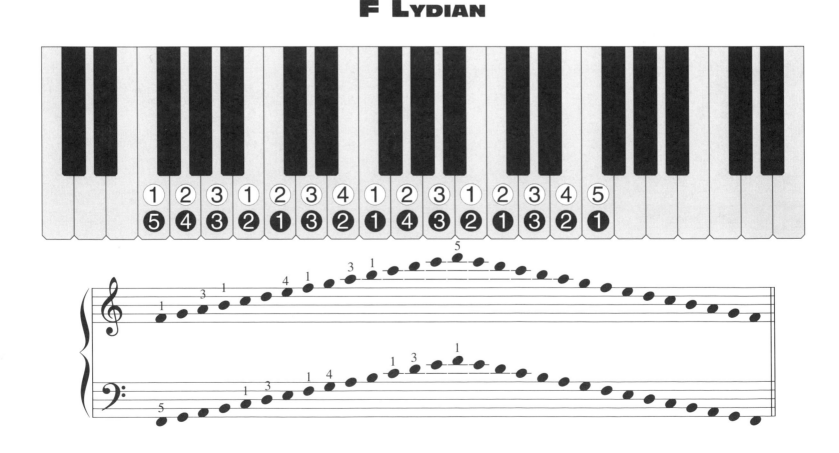

C LYDIAN

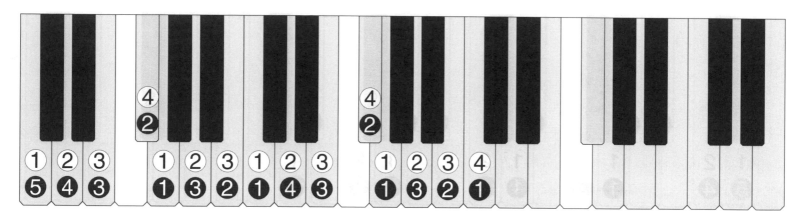

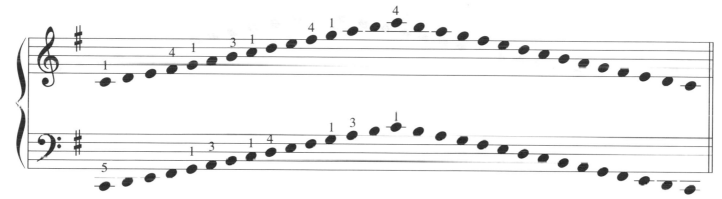

G LYDIAN

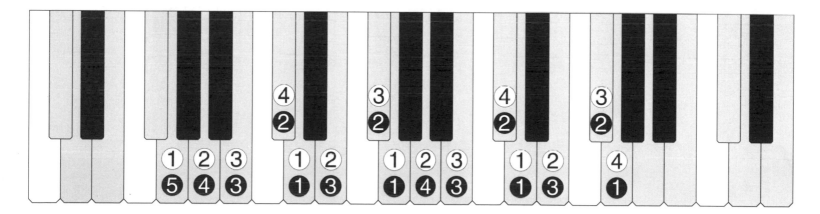

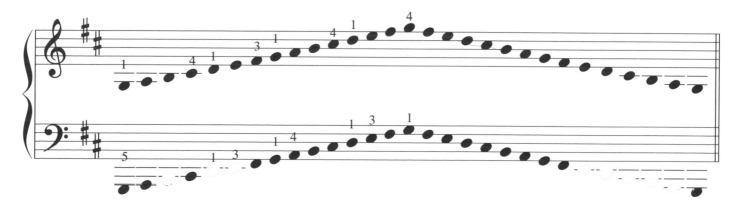

D Lydian

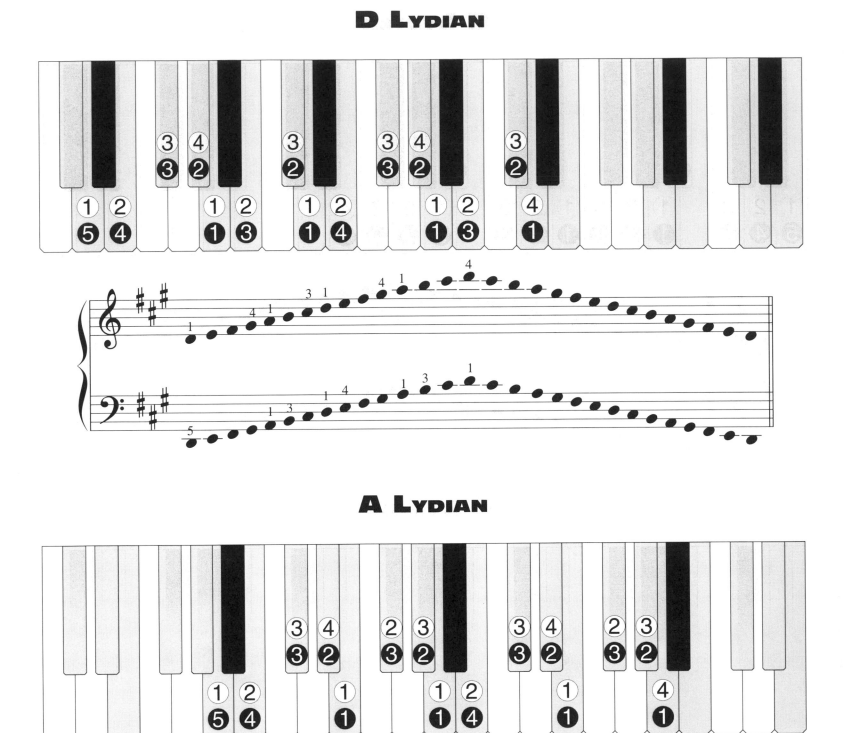

A Lydian

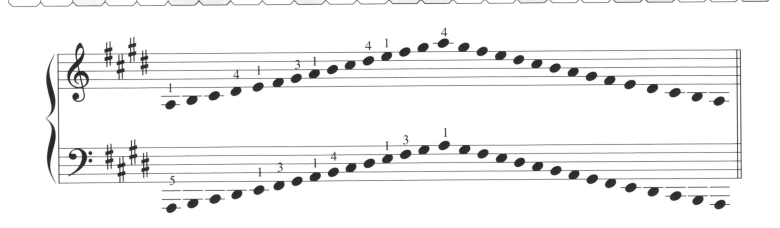

E LYDIAN

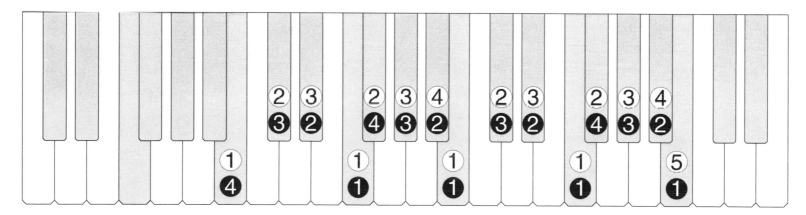

B LYDIAN

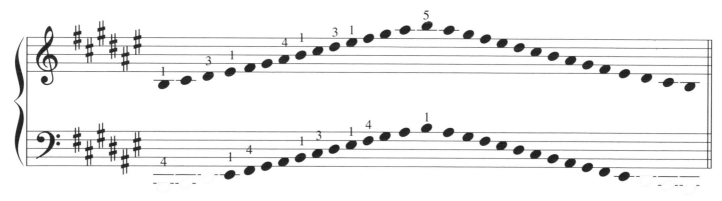

F# Lydian

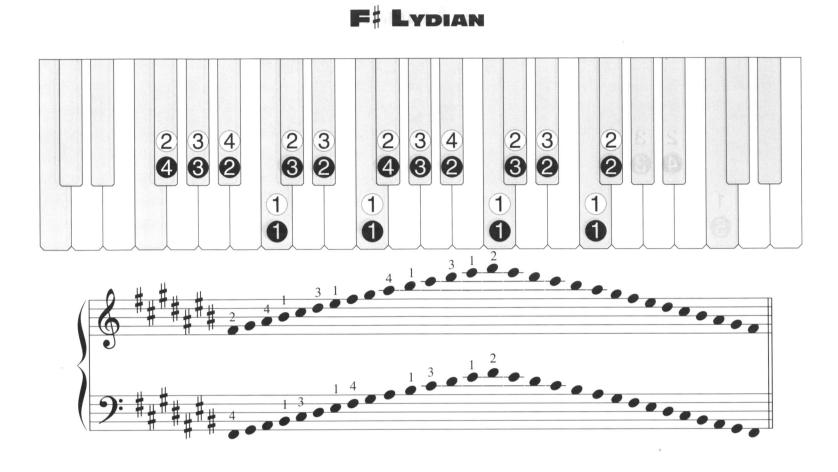

Bb Lydian

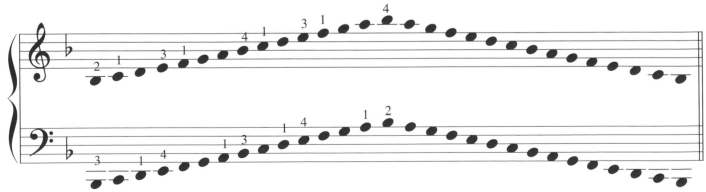

E♭ LYDIAN

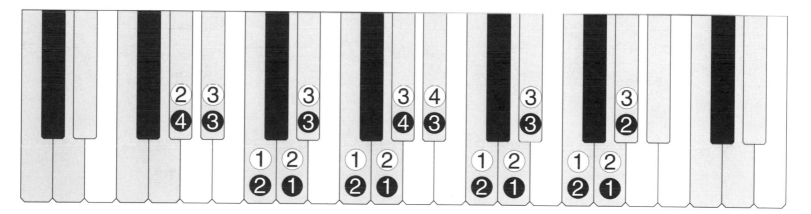

A♭ LYDIAN

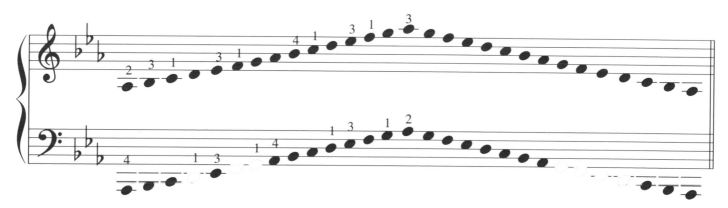

D♭ Lydian

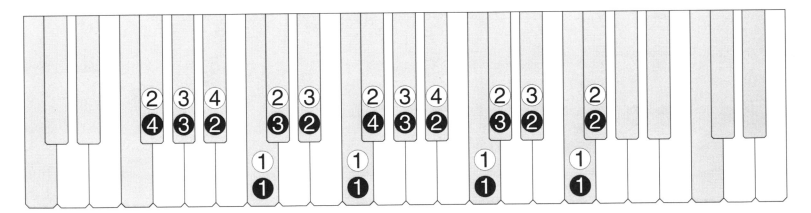

G♭ Lydian

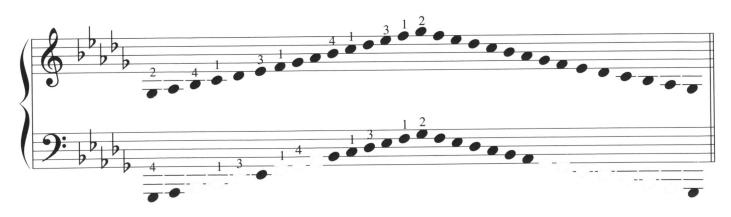

C♭ **LYDIAN**

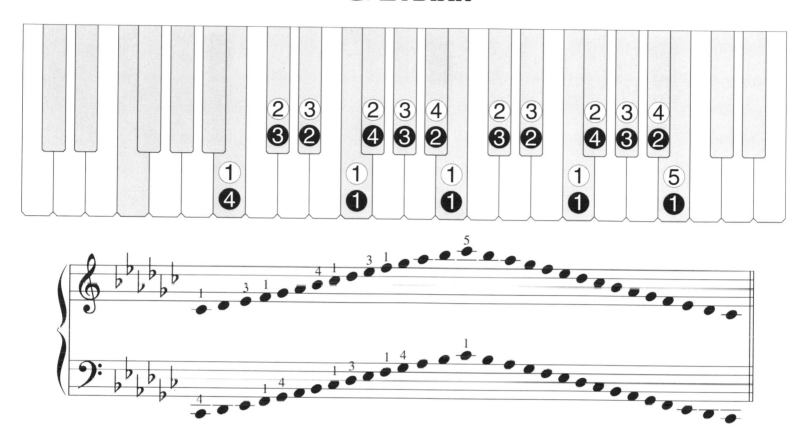

F♭ **LYDIAN**

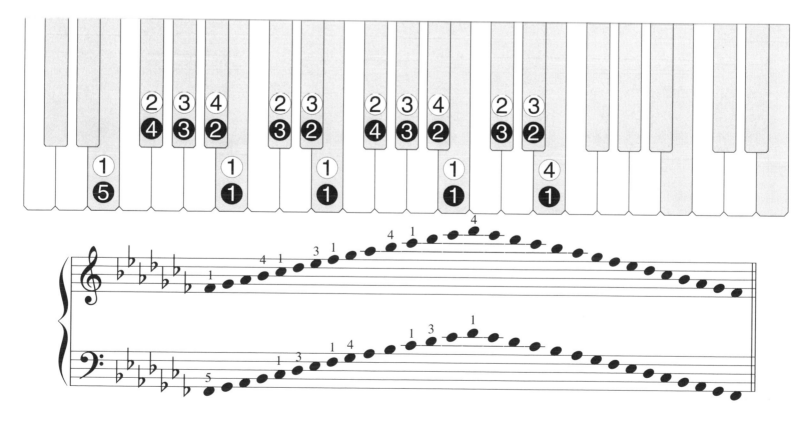

MIXOLYDIAN

The Mixolydian scale begins on the fifth degree of the major scale. The half steps of the Mixolydian mode occur between degrees three and four, and six and seven.

G Mixolydian scale

Like the Lydian scale, the Mixolydian scale has a major sound (except the seventh is flatted). You can hear the use of the Mixolydian mode in many folk and rock tunes.

Here are the basic triads of the Lydian scale, with major, minor, and diminished chords indicated.

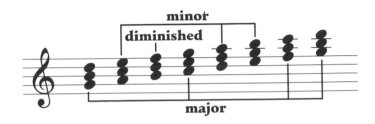

These musical works make significant use of the Mixolydian mode:
Piano Concerto #3 by Béla Bartók
Preludes for Piano by George Gershwin
Gymnopedie #2 by Erik Satie
I Wanna New Drug by Huey Lewis
The Heat is On by Glenn Frey

G MIXOLYDIAN

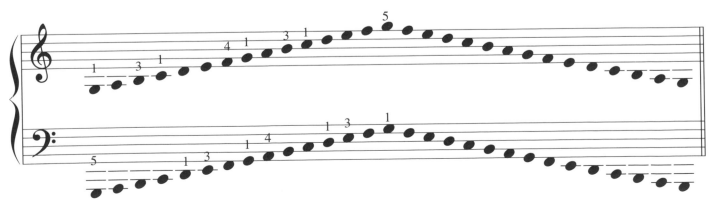

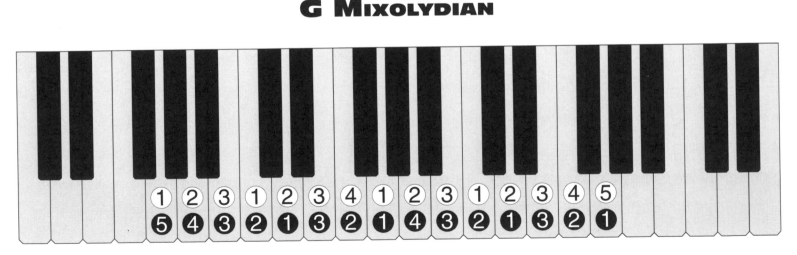

D MIXOLYDIAN

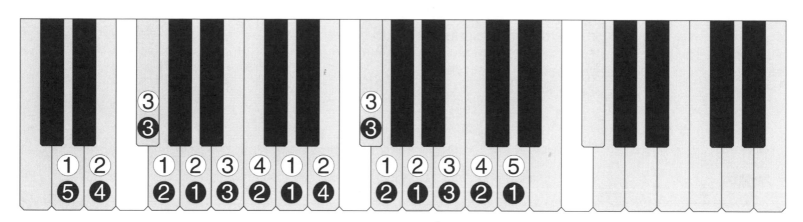

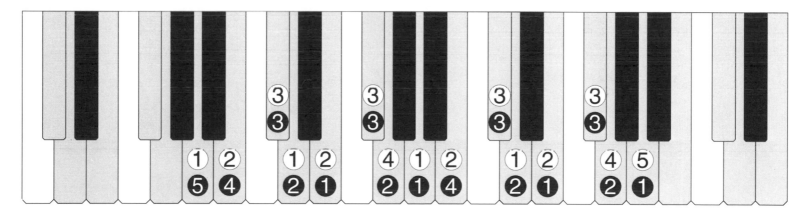

A MIXOLYDIAN

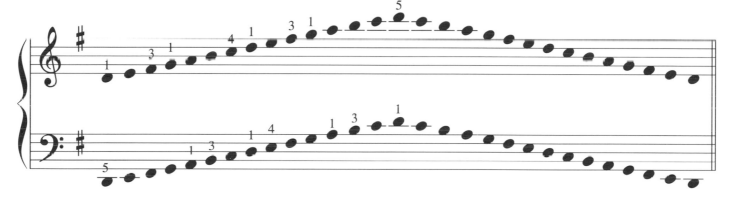

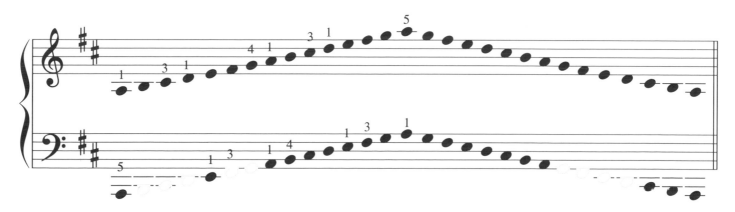

E Mixolydian

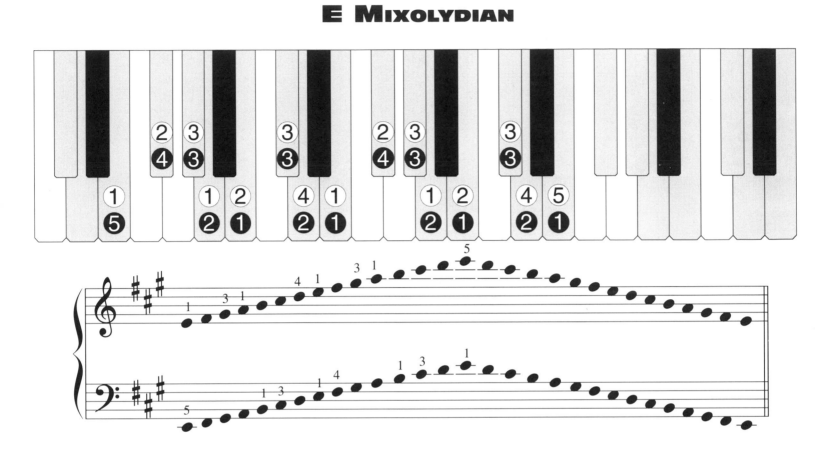

B Mixolydian

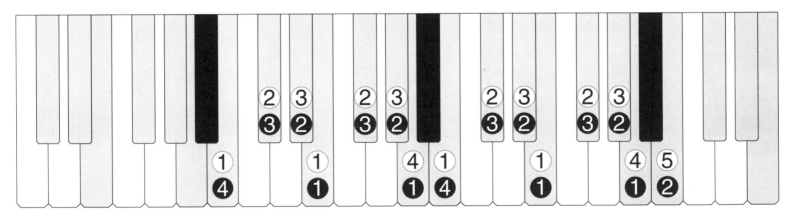

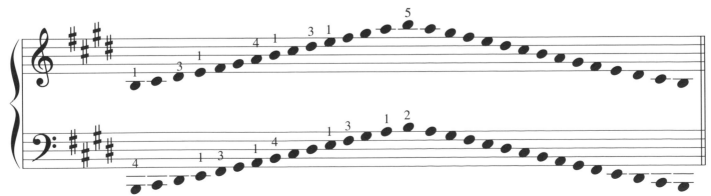

F♯ MIXOLYDIAN

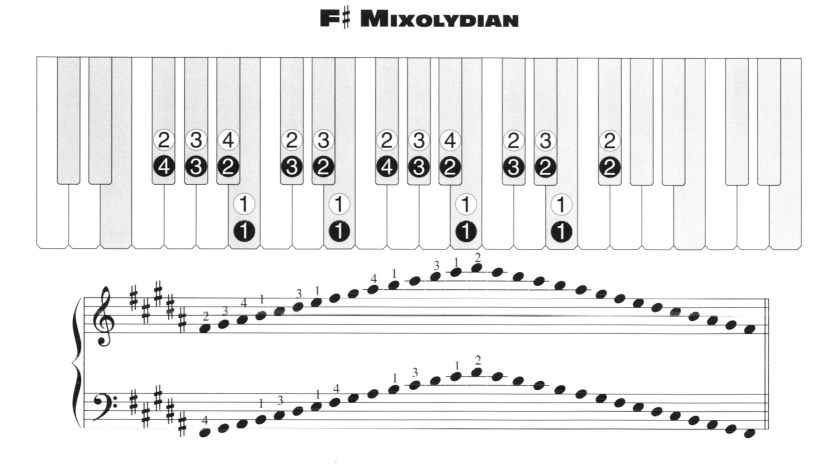

C♯ MIXOLYDIAN

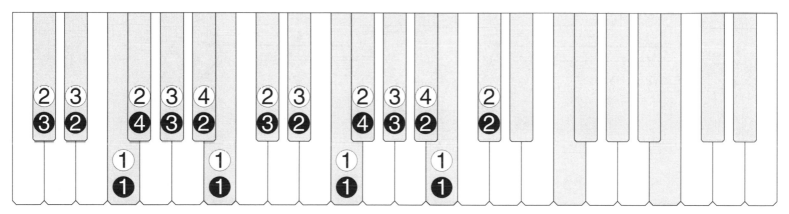

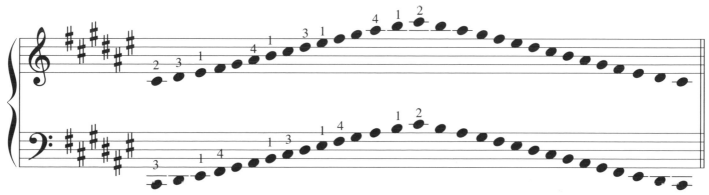

G♯ MIXOLYDIAN

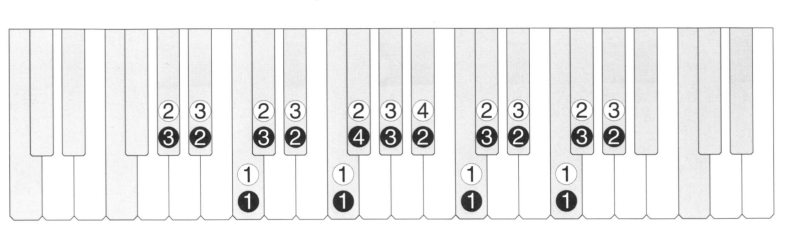

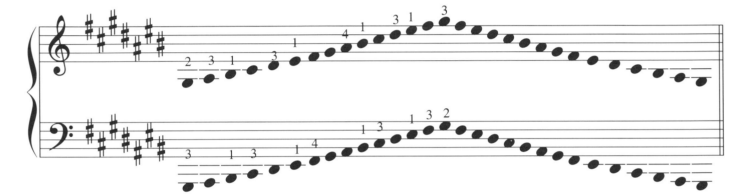

C MIXOLYDIAN

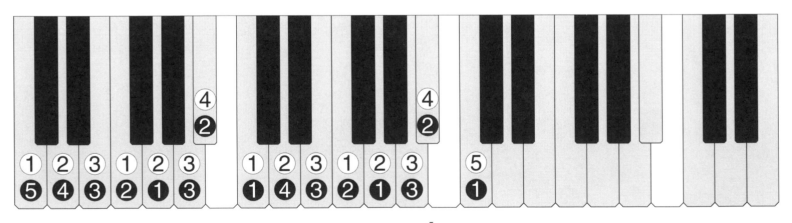

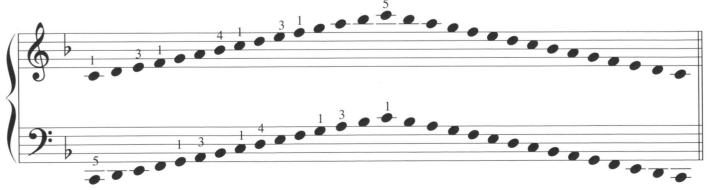

F MIXOLYDIAN

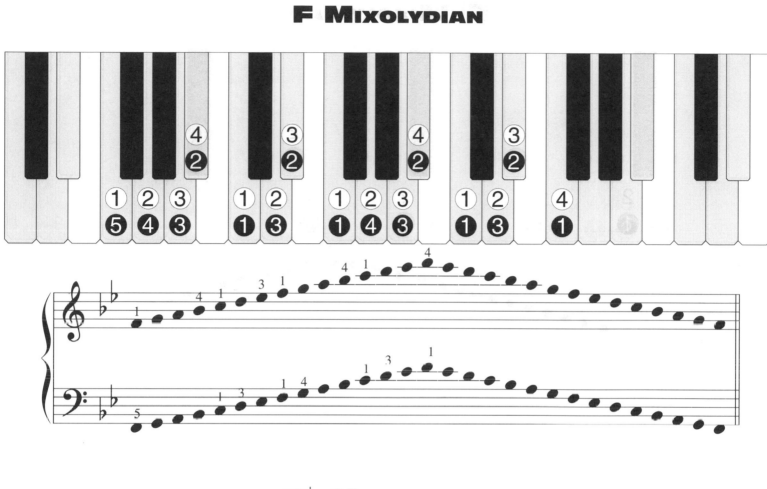

B♭ MIXOLYDIAN

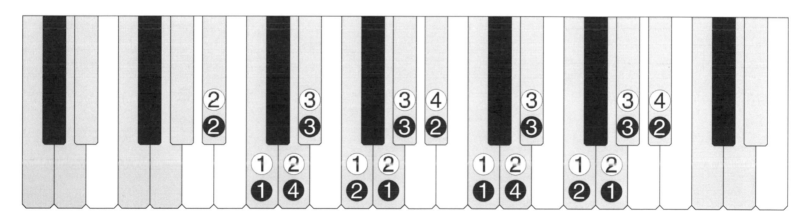

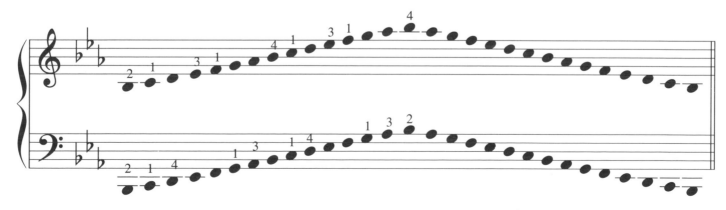

E♭ MIXOLYDIAN

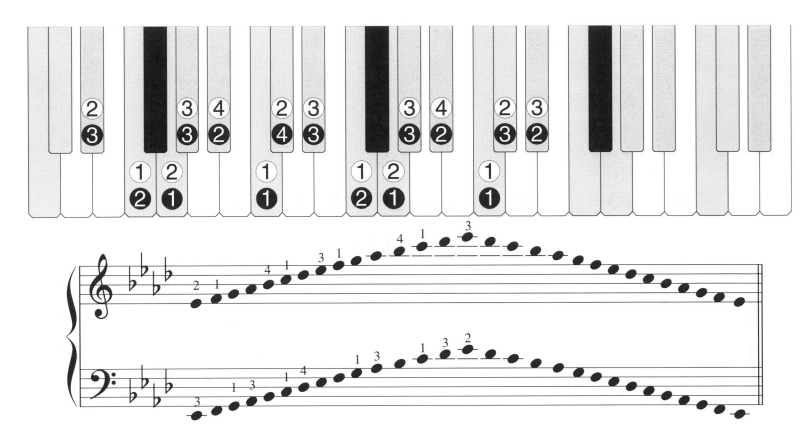

A♭ MIXOLYDIAN

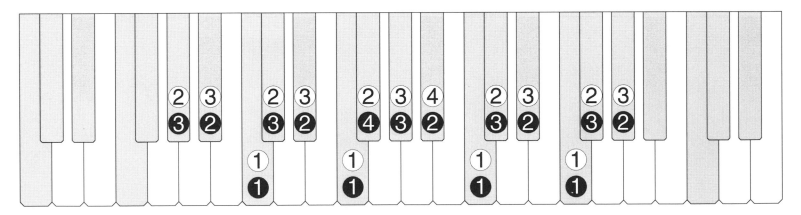

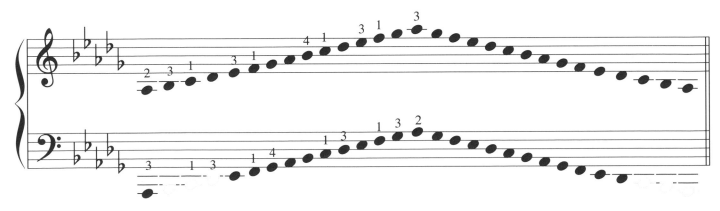

D♭ MIXOLYDIAN

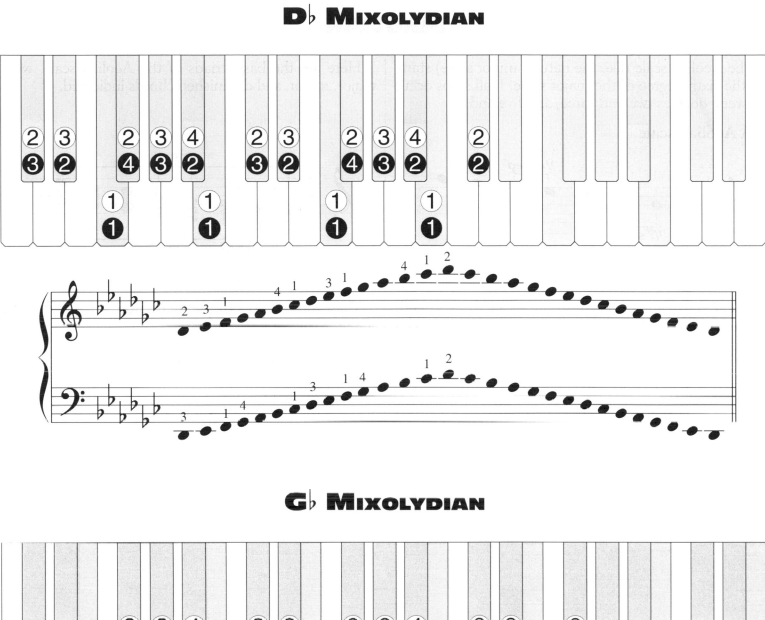

G♭ MIXOLYDIAN

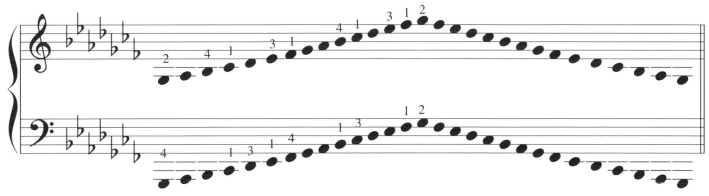

AEOLIAN

The Aeolian scale (like the natural minor scale) starts on the sixth degree of the major scale. Half steps occur between degrees two and three, and five and six.

A Aeolian scale

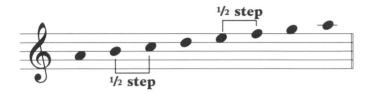

The Aeolian mode was introduced in the sixteenth century, considerably later than the previous four modes (which predominated throughout the middle ages).

Here are the basic triads of the Aeolian scale, with major, minor, and diminished chords indicated.

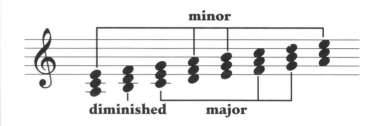

These musical works make significant use of the Aeolian mode:
Carmina Burana by Karl Orff
Four Saints in Three Acts by Virgil Thomson
Pines of Rome by Ottorina Respighi
Last in Line by Dio
Crazy Train by Ozzy Osbourne

A AEOLIAN

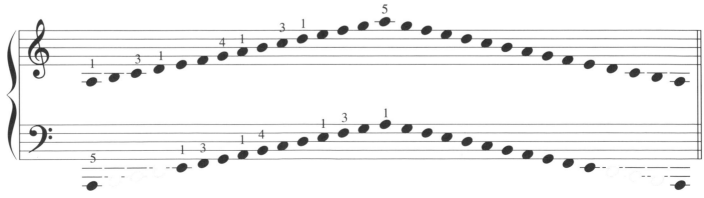

E AEOLIAN

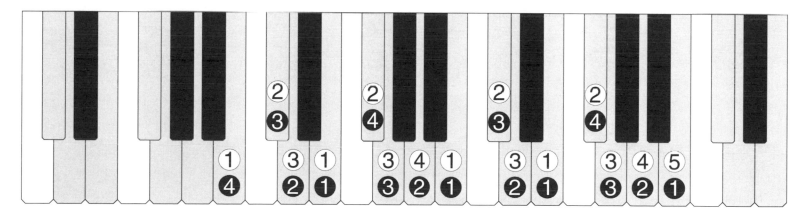

B AEOLIAN

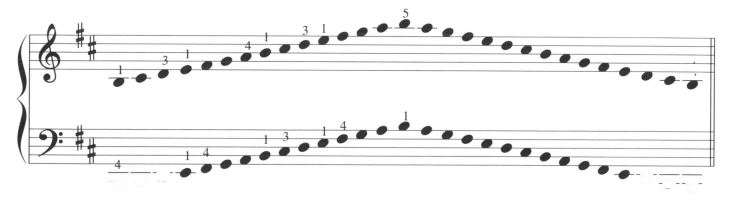

F♯ Aeolian

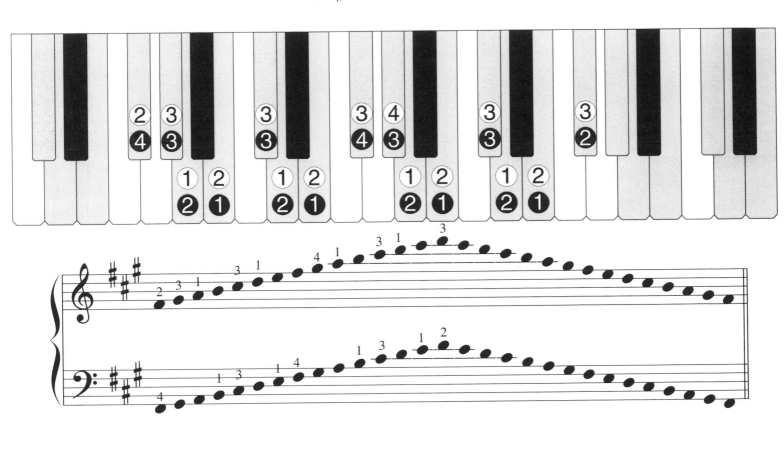

C♯ Aeolian

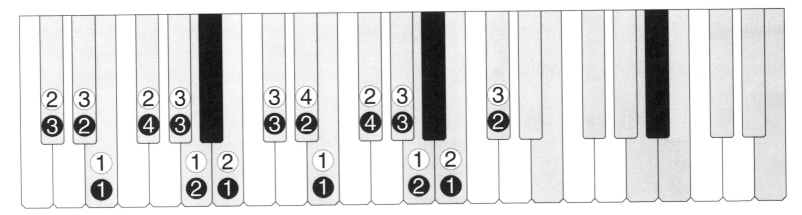

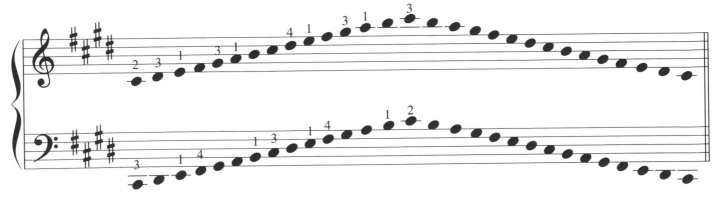

G♯ AEOLIAN

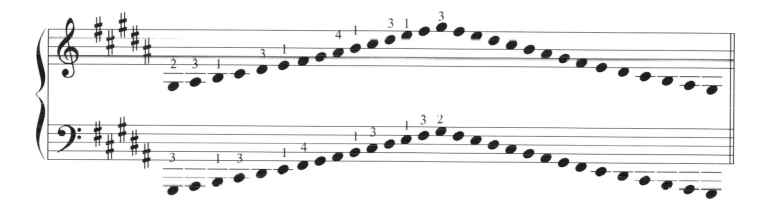

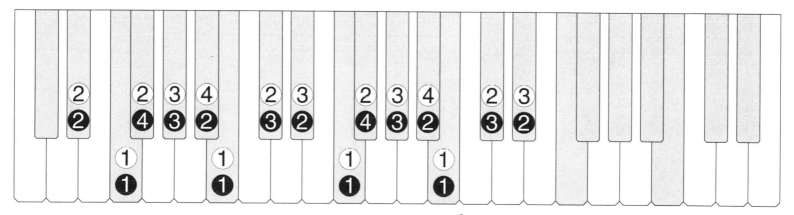

D♯ AEOLIAN

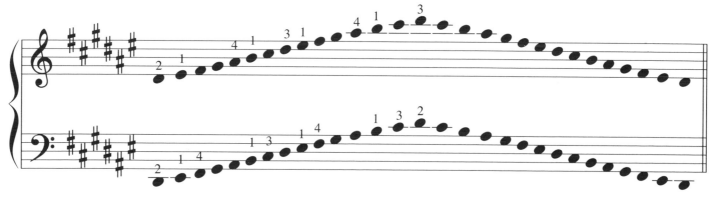

A♯ Aeolian

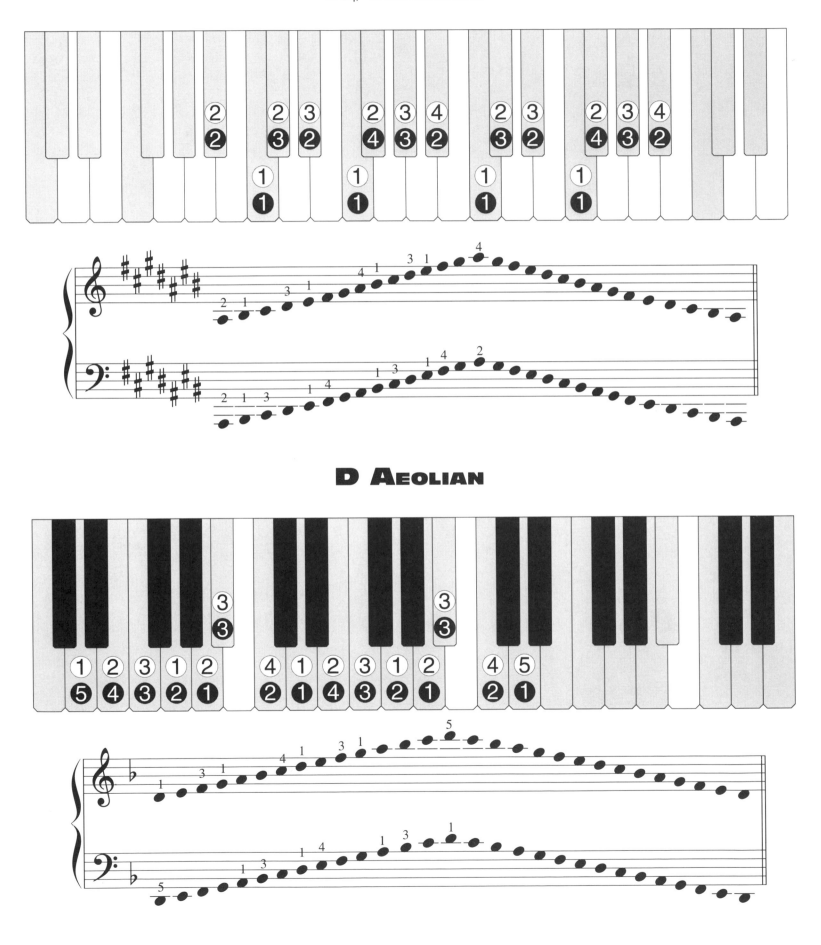

D Aeolian

G AEOLIAN

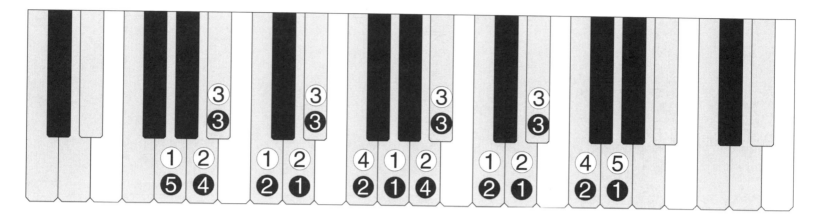

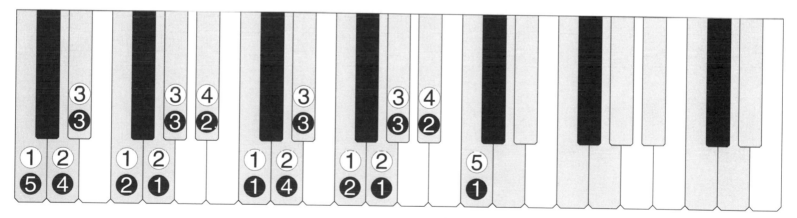

C AEOLIAN

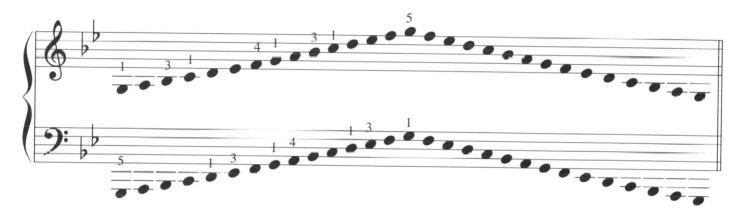

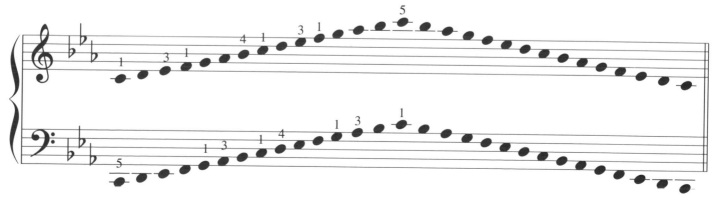

F Aeolian

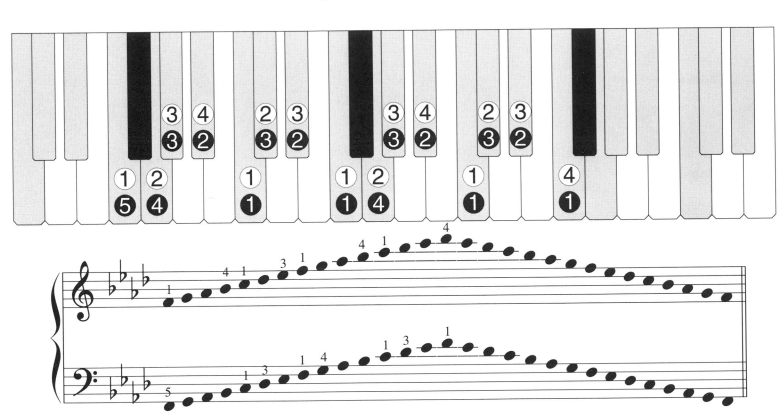

B♭ Aeolian

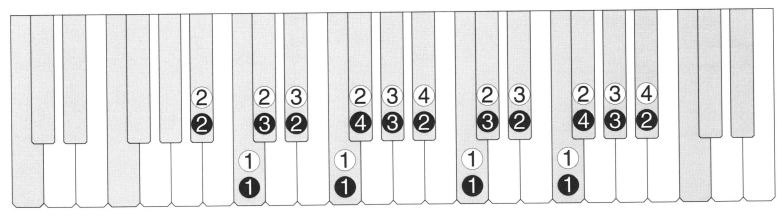

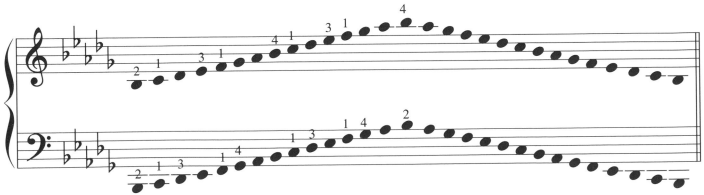

E♭ AEOLIAN

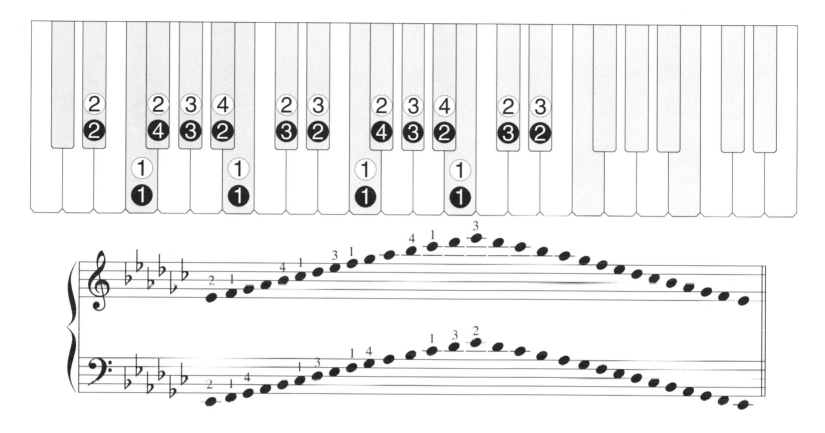

A♭ AEOLIAN

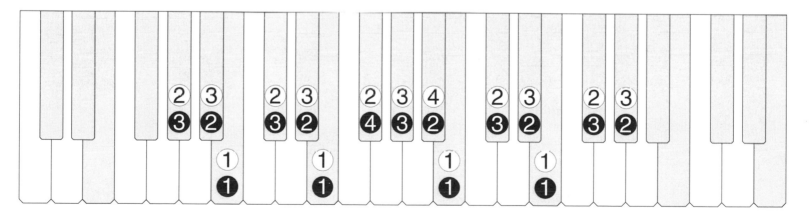

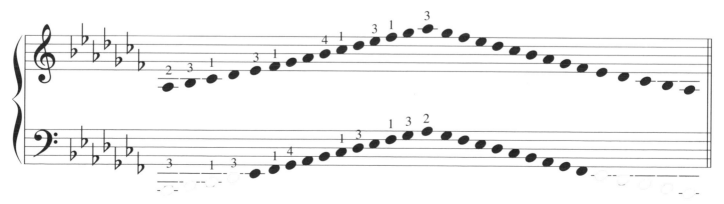

Locrian

The last mode is Locrian, which begins on the seventh degree of the major scale. Half steps occur between degrees one and two, and four and five.

B Locrian scale

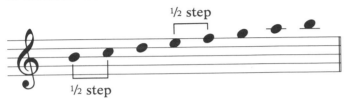

Because the Locrian scale is built around a diminished triad, its use is somewhat limited. You might hear a jazz player use this scale soloing over a minor 7♭5 (half diminished) chord, but it is rarely used in other types of music.

Here are the basic triads of the Locrian scale, with the major, minor, and diminished chords indicated.

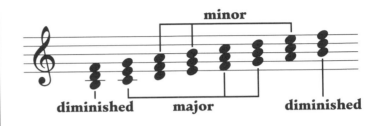

These musical works make significant use of the Locrian mode:
Mikrokosmos by Bela Bartók
Sonata for Flute, Viola, and Harp by Claude Debussy
Ludus Tonalis by Paul Hindemith

B Locrian

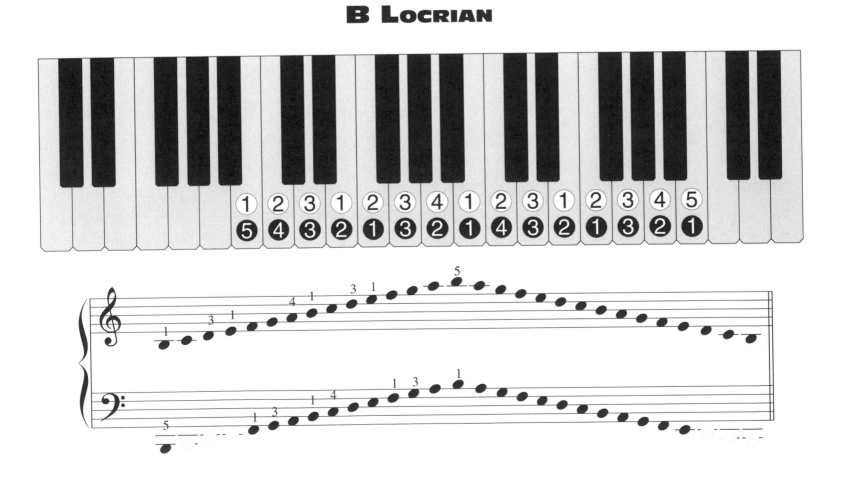

F♯ LOCRIAN

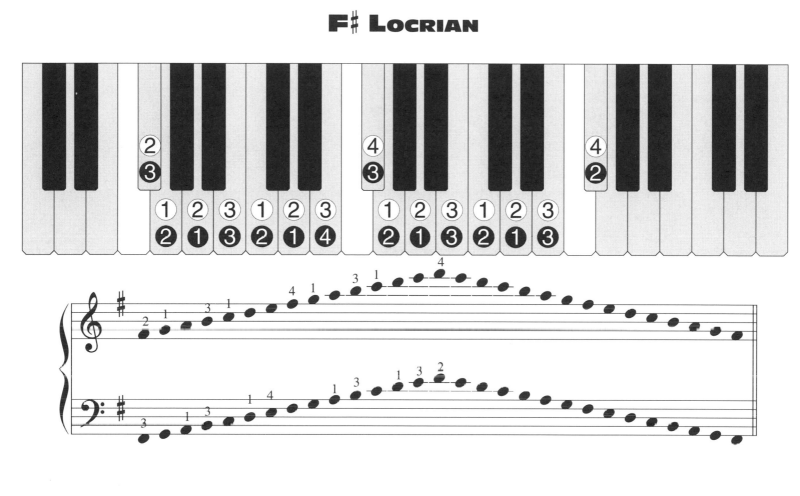

C♯ LOCRIAN

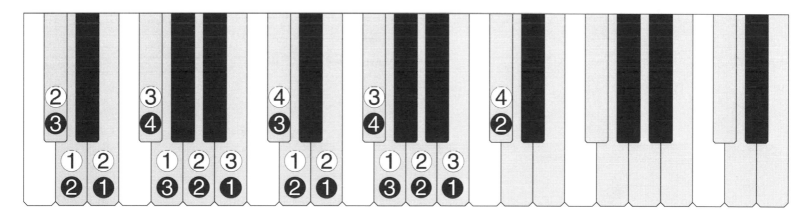

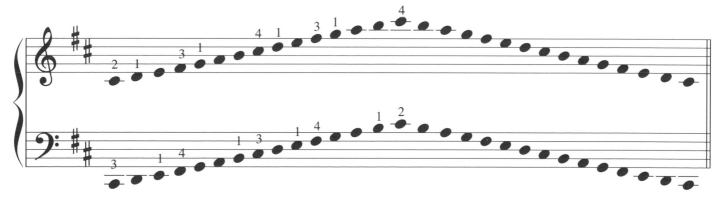

G# Locrian

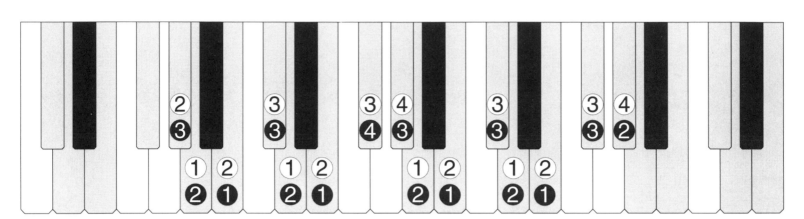

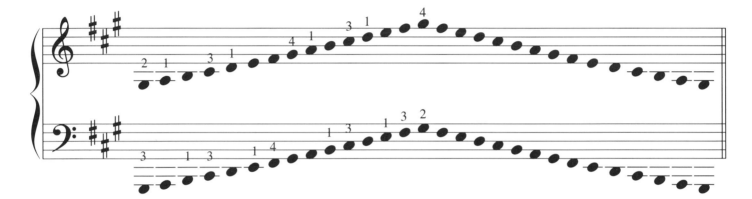

D# Locrian

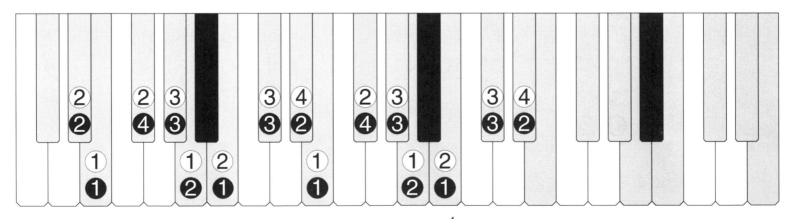

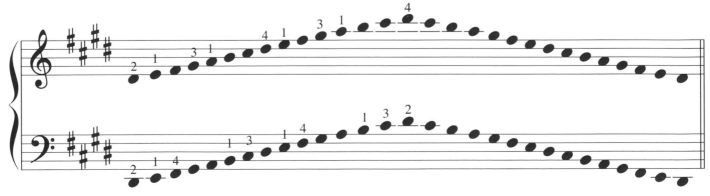

A♯ LOCRIAN

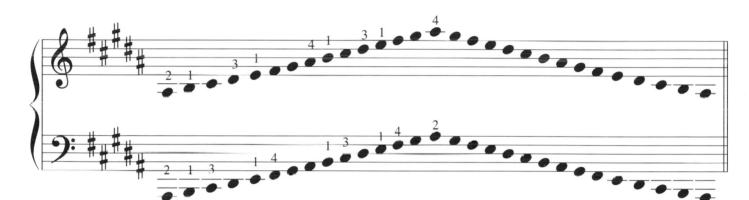

E♯ LOCRIAN

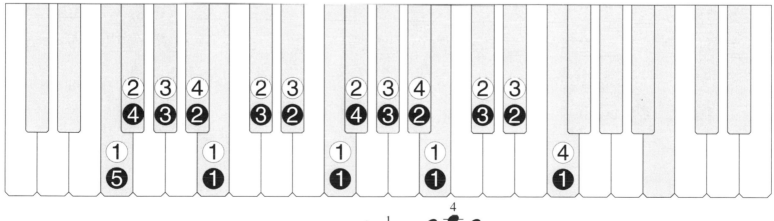

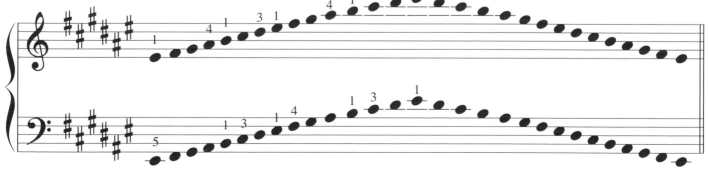

B♯ Locrian

E Locrian

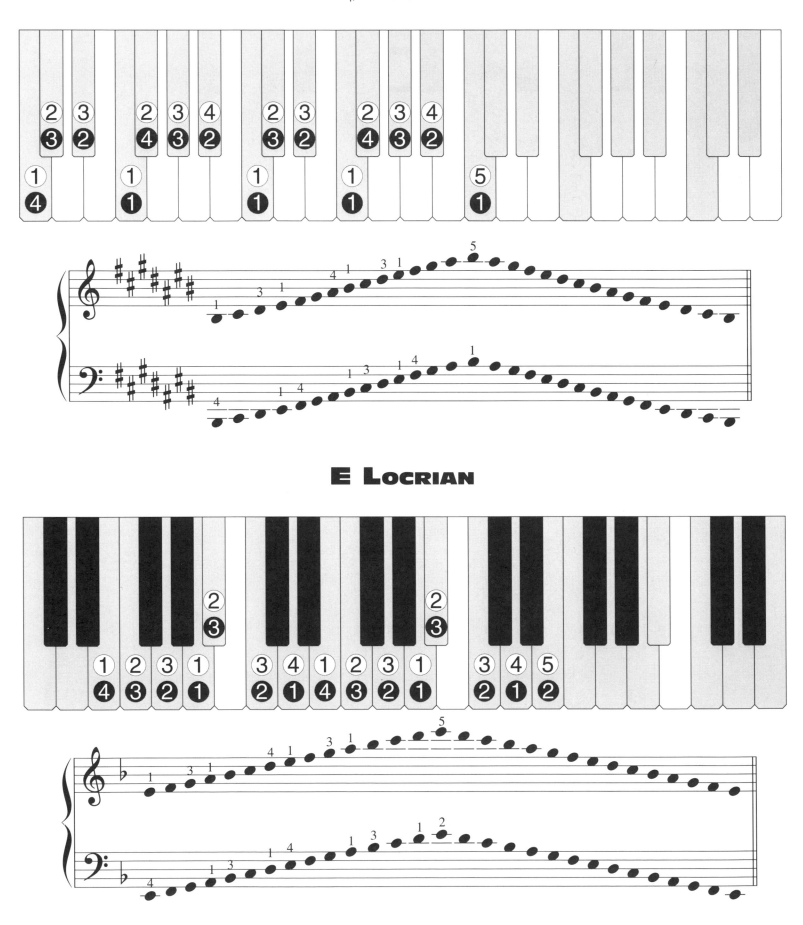

A LOCRIAN

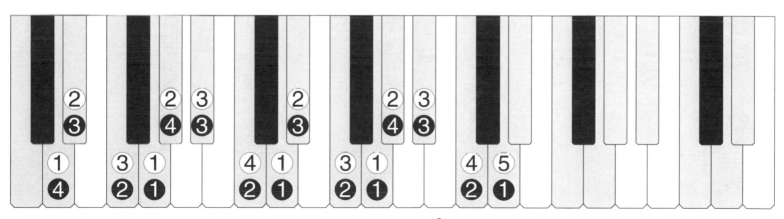

D LOCRIAN

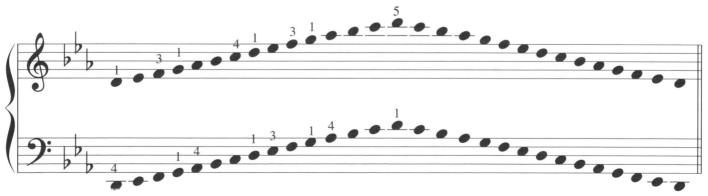

G Locrian

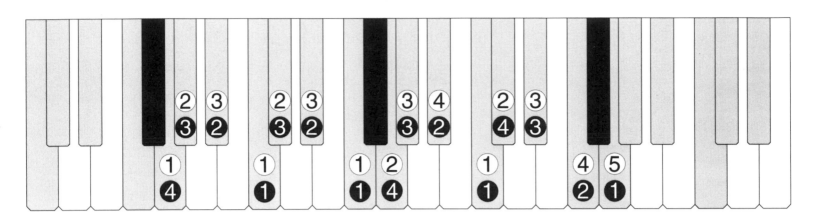

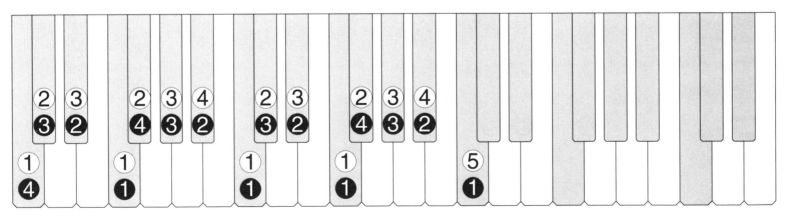

C Locrian

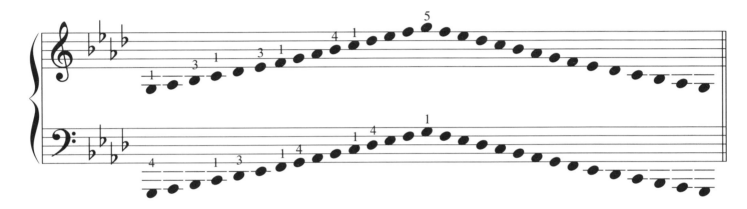

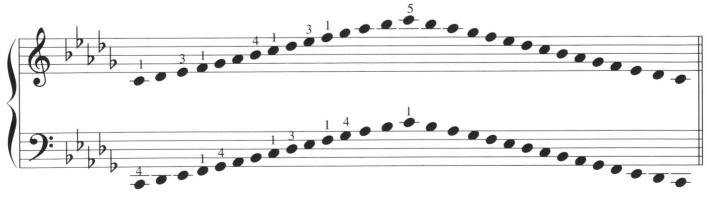

F LOCRIAN

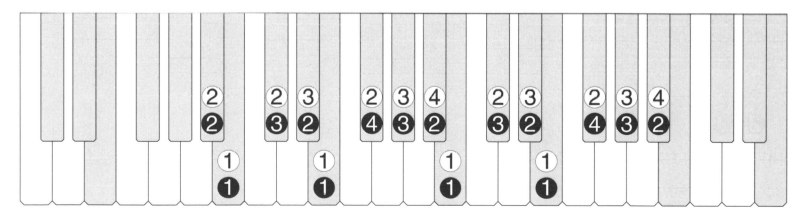

B♭ LOCRIAN

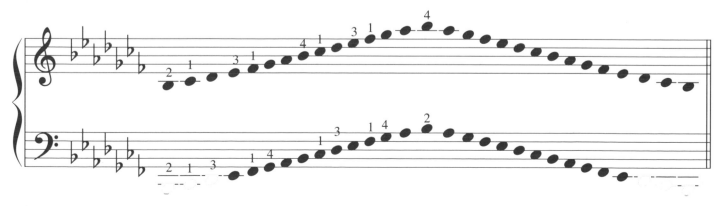